The Secret Life of
Victorian Houses

Authentic and Inspiring Interiors and What They Reveal

Elan and Susan Zingman-Leith
Photographs by Tim Fields

Viking Studio

For Eli—E. & S.Z.-L.
To Karen, Alec & Taylor—T.F.

(Page 1) *Reflections of domestic life in a Victorian bedroom.*
(Pages 2–3) *A cottage-style child's bedroom with doll furniture.*
(Page 4) *A Gothic Revival entrance with picturesque Moorish door.*

VIKING STUDIO
Published by the Penguin Group
Penguin Putnam Inc., 375 Hudson Street,
New York, New York 10014, U.S.A.
Penguin Books Ltd, 27 Wrights Lane,
London W8 5TZ, England
Penguin Books Australia Ltd, Ringwood,
Victoria, Australia
Penguin Books Canada Ltd, 10 Alcorn Avenue,
Toronto, Ontario, Canada M4V 3B2
Penguin Books (N.Z.) Ltd, 182-190 Wairau Road,
Auckland 10, New Zealand

Penguin Books Ltd, Registered Offices:
Harmondsworth, Middlesex, England

First published in the United States of America by
Elliott & Clark Publishing 1993
Published by Viking Studio 2000

10 9 8 7 6 5 4 3 2 1

The Library of Congress has cataloged the hardcover
edition as follows:
Fields, Tim, 1962–
The secret life of Victorian houses / photography by
Tim Fields; Text by Elan and Susan Zingman-Leith.
p.   cm.
Includes bibliographic references.
ISBN 1-880216-10-8 (hc)
        1-14-029461-9 (pbk)
1. Architecture, Domestic–United States.
2. Architecture, Victorian United States. 3. Interior
decoration–United States–History–19th century.
4. Victoriana in interior decoration. I. Zingman-Leith,
Elan, 1951– II. Zingman-Leith, Susan, 1950–
III. Title
NA7207.F54   1993
728'.0973'09034–dc20   93-12129

Printed in China

TABLE OF CONTENTS

INTRODUCTION

THIS BOOK BEGAN WITH Tim Fields' interest in photographing Victorian interiors. He visited our bed and breakfast to see the parlor and the bedrooms, and we fell to talking about his future book. Since we are an extremely chatty couple, we started telling him about how mistaken most people are in their image of Victorian life and how houses could really reveal a lot about social history. We spoke for hours about servants and immigrants, mass production and the Industrial Revolution, architecture and style. We ended up writing the book while he started taking the wonderful, evocative photographs you'll see in the following pages.

We believe that any subject—sports, literature, science, music, furniture, food, or anything else—can be a key to understanding how people lived in the past. Social history is not treaties and treatises; it is how people lived and ate and dressed, how they went to work and went to sleep.

This book is about the Victorian era, basically the second half of the nineteenth century. It looks at Victorian houses and tries to explain why they are the way they are, what they can tell us about how people lived in them, and what Victorian life was really like.

The modern image of Victorian life as all ruffles and roses, teacakes and laces is a lie. That image is a nostalgic look back at a past that never existed. The Victorian era was a time of wrenching changes for most people, a rate of change so fast and furious that it has yet to be equaled in modern life. We are going to look at the evidence left in surviving Victorian houses.

We will not just explore daily life, but the daily life of a new class of people—the middle class—the managers, clerks, and white-collar workers of post-Civil War, industrial, urban America. This is not everyone's story. New immigrants were generally excluded and lived in urban slums or newly

Queen Victoria is presiding in porcelain over a sideboard full of china at the Ebenezer Maxwell Mansion in Philadelphia. How appropriate that she should look down from a machine-made Renaissance Revival sideboard, surrounded by factory-made dishes, the inventions of her reign.

opened frontiers. Native Americans were usually excluded by racial and cultural prejudice. African Americans participated in the rise of the middle class for a brief time between the end of the Civil War and the repeal of reconstruction in the 1870s. After the repeal, Jim Crow laws, lynching, and the Ku Klux Klan excluded African Americans from most of the rewards of the Industrial Revolution. The story is an important one, however, because the values of the late nineteenth century became our modern mores and affect all of us to this day.

> *This next thing particularly noticeable is that everybody seems in a hurry to catch a train. This is a state of things which is not favourable to poetry or romance. Had Romeo or Juliet been in a constant state of anxiety about trains, or had their minds been agitated by the question of return-tickets, Shakespeare could not have given us those lovely balcony scenes which are so full of poetry and pathos.*
>
> —*Impressions of America*, 1883, Oscar Wilde

THE DINING ROOM

THE NEW ERA OF SELF-CONTROL

All human history attests
That happiness for man,—the hungry
sinner!—
Since Eve ate apples, much depends on
dinner.
—*Don Juan,* Lord Byron (1788-1824)

(Pages 8-9) Jay Gould bought Lyndhurst in 1880, thus purchasing the style of barons and earls to ornament his fortune made from Western Union, the New York "el," and Union Pacific railroad. This is as high-style a Gothic dining room as can be found in America and, of course, completely unlike a real Gothic hall—no dogs, no smell, no garbage on the floor. (Facing) The dining room in the Victoria Mansion represents an extraordinary effort in 1859 to bring the taste and refinement of an Italian Renaissance villa to the wilderness of Portland, Maine.

DINING ROOMS ARE PERHAPS the best evidence of the revolution that took place in society in the middle of the nineteenth century. The Industrial Revolution not only made all the furniture, dishes, and silver plate possible, but also created a new class of people to use them. Early in the nineteenth century, the existence of a dining room at all was the mark of the gentry. Ordinary folk cooked and ate and lived in all-purpose rooms. The landed gentry of the South and the merchant shippers of the North might boast a separate room just for eating, but they represented only a very small part of the population. By the 1860s, a separate dining room was considered *de rigueur* for even a cottage, and eating "in the kitchen" was thought of as rustic and rude. Middle-class people could even aspire to a sideboard in the dining room, by far the most expensive piece of furniture in the house.

By the 1870s, for the first time, most Americans lived in cities rather than on farms. The change began in the 1820s with the development of the Erie Canal, the steam engine, and the railroad. New transportation and coal

from Pennsylvania sped up the Industrial Revolution in the 1850s, and the Civil War subsidized it in the 1860s. Someone had to manage the companies that owned the factories, clerks had to record the activity of the manufactories, and salesmen had to market the products. Suddenly, a whole new class of people developed—white-collar workers. They didn't work with their hands, and they made a predictable salary. They could afford to copy the life and ape the manners of the gentry of their parents' generation. The same Industrial Revolution and urbanization that provided the middle class with an income also produced cheap versions of the dishes, cutlery, and plate that were the mark of gentility in the early nineteenth century.

People in the late nineteenth century often remarked on how much manners had improved in the past fifty years. Perhaps because the new middle class was just establishing its gentility, they outdid by far the real gentry of the early nineteenth century. In the 1820s, a gentleman's dinner would consist of a *table d'hôte*, i.e., all the courses would be laid out on the table at once. Soup, fish, vegetables, meat, relishes, and desserts would be waiting on the table as the guests came in. Guests would choose and sample the food, pass platters and plates, and help themselves and their neighbors. They would eat with their knives or sometimes a fork. At a simple man's table, they would share plates and eat out of serving dishes. At a particularly lavish repast, everything might be cleared halfway through the meal and another round of meats, side dishes, and sweets brought in. After dinner, the ladies would retire to the drawing room, and the men would urinate in the pots stored behind the doors of the sideboard.

By the late nineteenth century, even a middle-class dinner was much more orderly and controlled. The *table d'hôte* was replaced by "Russian service" where each course was served by gloved servants who brought each guest measured portions on a plate as in a modern restaurant. In the

(Facing) By the late nineteenth century, silver plate and china were well within the reach of successful middle-class folk. This sideboard is loaded with such treasures and ornamented by carved animal heads, reminding the diner of the hunt for the evening's food. In this refined setting, however, dinner was more likely to have been ordered from the grocer.

old days, when guests helped each other to food and table manners were relaxed and intimate, there was no strict division between served and servant, perhaps because no one had to prove his worthiness for his station in life—he was born to it. The gentry were gentry and common folk were common, and that's the way it had always been. By the late nineteenth century, everyone's station in life was in flux, and who you were depended on your income and your manners. The need for control grew in direct proportion to the increasing chaos of modern urban life.

In the first place they satisfy themselves that they are helps, *not* servants—*that they are going to work with (not for) Mr. so and so, not going to service—they call him and his wife their* employers, *not their master and mistress.*

—*Civilized America,* 1859, Thomas Colley Grattan

When the guests filed into a Victorian dinner in the late nineteenth century, they found small menus on the table describing the food they would be served. Servants set and removed a plate for every course, and no one used fingers to touch the food. There were special forks and ladles and knives for every conceivable food: oyster ladles and forks; tomato servers; fish knives and forks; cake knives and servers and forks; different spoons for clear soup, for cream soup, for dessert, for fruit, for breakfast coffee, for dinner coffee, and for tea. The volume and variety of silver-plated flatware and hollowware would baffle any modern diner. But to the Victorian, knowing the code of the correct fork was all-important proof of gentility and all that separated the "right" people from laborers, immigrants, and vagabonds. No one at dinner passed food or served his neighbor; the difference between servant and served was so important because the roles could

The dining room at the Windward House in Cape May, New Jersey, shows the real taste of Victorian homeowners. A tapestry of pussycats peering over a fence and a wreath made of dear, departed grandma's hair ornament the walls. If only they had known about Elvis painted on velvet, how happy they would have been.

be reversed by a simple change in fortune. The host was in complete control of the guests' meal by predetermining the order of the courses and the quantity of the food. After dinner, the ladies retired to the drawing room, and the men tarried over their cigars and port. The little doors in the sideboard now held places for wine and linens, not chamber pots.

What is so amazing about Victorian table manners is how successful they were. We may no longer use all the cutlery, but we have internalized their whole system of suppressing bodily functions and being proper. In the early nineteenth century, diners still had to be reminded not to blow their noses on the tablecloth, not to spit food back into serving dishes, not to pick their teeth with their knives, and not to urinate in front of ladies. By the late nineteenth century, etiquette books no longer had to give that kind of advice because it was assumed that people knew enough to control themselves in public. The self-contained, modern, discreet person was invented in the late nineteenth century as a reaction to the loss of control inherent in modern, anonymous city life. The noteworthy element is not how quaint the Victorians were or how different, but how much more like us they are than any other people before them.

To really appreciate the revolution in eating in the late nineteenth century, it would help to see a Victorian dining room with its pantry fully stocked and its food on the table. The nineteenth century saw the introduction and spread of brand-name foods, prepackaging, logos, and graphic labels. Before the Victorian era, food was either raised or grown at home or bought in bulk. The local general store or grocer had large sacks of sugar, beans, and flours; barrels of molasses and pickles; as well as spices such as pepper, cloves, and allspice. The grocer measured and weighed his wares into the customer's containers and kept a tab, billing his accounts once a month. Milk, eggs, and fowl were purchased from a country farmer who brought them to market or, more likely, from a city dairyman who kept cows and chickens in town.

In the middle of the nineteenth century, the quality of foods often got a lot worse. Railroads and urbanization supported the growth of the food business. Flour was milled closer to the source or closer to cheap transportation rather than closer to the consumer. It was commonly extended by unscrupulous companies with a measure of chalk dust or plaster. Tea was often stretched with iron filings, a profitable ingredient for a product sold by weight. Milk was often skimmed of valuable cream and sold as whole. Even when it wasn't, city cows often lived in multistory brick barns, were fed on rotten silage, and infected with tuberculosis. These consumptive Camilles of the cow world hardly gave the thick, white milk that Americans were used to. New York City's milk was most often described as watery and bluish. By the late nineteenth century, there were strong reactions to the declining quality of food.

(Facing) Here at the Henry Bowen House, the rich texture of Anaglypta and Lyncrusta-Walton wall coverings set off sumptuous Sèvres china.

THE HEALTH FOOD MOVEMENT
AND HOME ECONOMICS

The present ... takes pride in its ability to produce ever larger quantities of food—pasteurized, homogenized, sterilized, frozen, or otherwise reduced to an infant's standard of tastelessness.

—Lewis Mumford (1895–1990)

DURING THE 1870S, Dr. John Harvey Kellogg was hired to manage the Western Health Reform Institute which he renamed the Battle Creek Sanitarium. He believed in crispy foods to clean the teeth, uncooked fruit as God made it, and bran to encourage evacuation. He said, "Bran does not irritate, it titillates." His first commercial product was called Granola, but there was another product already on the market called Granula so he changed the name to Granose and sold 100,000 pounds in the first year. One of his patients was Charles Post. After nine months Post still had his ulcers, but he had learned the joy of food marketing. In 1895 he invented Postum, a coffee substitute, and, soon thereafter, a dry cereal called Elijah's Manna. As grocers objected to the blasphemy, he renamed it Grape Nuts. Soon after he followed with Post-Toasties.

Kellogg prescribed a diet high in grains and low in the ubiquitous salt pork on which most Americans subsisted. He was so successful that he packaged his corn flakes and advertised them heavily, urging brand-name loyalty as an assurance of purity. Post marketed his Grape Nuts and Post-Toasties in the same way—with a distinctive logo, testimonials from doctors and patients, and factory packaging. The National Biscuit Company put up billboards across America assuring consumers that "You Need a

Biscuit" (Uneeda Biscuit) was packaged in a moisture-proof wrapping to ensure a pure, untainted, crisp product.

At the same time, the Reverend Sylvester Graham was an evangelist for whole-wheat flour and developed a sweetened whole-wheat cracker (the Graham cracker) that was supposed to keep the consumer not only healthy, but also moral. Graham was both a Presbyterian minister and an agent of the Pennsylvania Temperance Society and marketed his new cracker to board-ing schools as a suppressant of masturbation in boys. This was certainly creative advertising that even a modern advertising executive would admire.

The greatest contributor among these health-food pioneers was Gail Borden. City people were being poisoned by tainted milk every day. Borden discovered that by evaporating much of the water from milk and canning the result, the milk didn't have to be refrigerated. The cows could live a healthy, country life while the consumers could stay far away in the city, hence Borden's famous slogan for Carnation milk: "from contented cows."

The other strong influence on late nineteenth-century eating was the home-economics movement. Well-educated, middle-class, nonimmigrant women not only created a profession of their own, but also sought to Americanize urban slum dwellers. Home economists and social workers tried to teach immigrant women about nutrition and tried to wean them away from the "hot," spicy cuisine of their homelands. The favorite foods of the home economics movement were gelatin salads and boiled dressings. A blanket of white sauce covering a slab of boneless protein was the ideal

The dappled light of Gothic stained glass falls across the table at Lyndhurst. The elegance and refinement of manners in this dining room were, in fact, brand new, developed in the previous forty years.

dish. Salads were orderly, encased, cool, and controllable rather than hot, sloppy, and sensuous. Jello, after all, is a Victorian product invented during the 1890s by the Genesee Pure Food Company of Leroy, New York. This change in cuisine was not all one-way bullying. Cookbooks like Fannie Farmer's and Mrs. Beeton's, as well as manners books like Emily Post's, were eagerly bought by immigrant women who wanted to fit into American culture. These books gave advice on food, eating, and household management to Europeans who wanted to know how things were "done" in America.

THE PARLOR

A NEW ROLE FOR WOMEN

"Will you walk into my parlor?" said
the spider to the fly;
"'Tis the prettiest little parlor that
ever you did spy."

—"The Spider and the Fly," Mary Howitt (1799-1888)

(Pages 22-23) While the outside of the Victoria Mansion is an Italianate villa, the parlor was considered a woman's room and got the full Louis XV, Rococo Revival treatment. The Aubusson rug, cabriole legs on the furniture, and pastel color scheme implied that the mistress of the house was as elegant as Marie Antoinette. (Facing) No prisoner to a single historic style, the parlor at Wilderstein features French classical wall ornament, Turkish-style comfy chairs, a Japanese screen, oriental carpets, and a Chippendale chair.

THE DECORATION OF THE PARLOR and the choice and arrangement of the furniture reflect the changing role of women in the nineteenth century. Woman as the embodiment of purity and high moral virtue was a theme which nineteenth-century popular culture adopted with obsessive fervor. Before the middle of the century the image of woman was what it had been since the Middle Ages. She was the daughter of Eve, the embodiment of wantonness. Before the Industrial Revolution, misogynic literature always pictured women as less than human beings, closer to animals, and less able to control their lusts by exercise of their intellect or moral powers.

By the 1880s, the myth of the pure Victorian woman was fully formed, and the transformation of woman's image was complete. Late nineteenth-century reformers wrote that women had no libido; that, in fact, it was replaced by a "maternal instinct," and that women only consented to sex to please their husbands and to have children. Women were also said to be the kinder, gentler gender with higher moral standards and greater self-control. Men were thought of as smarter and more competent but more lustful and "primitive" with less ability to control their passions.

Two dramatic changes took place in gender roles in the middle of the nineteenth century. Not only did men and women trade places as the moral force in society, but also the accepted roles of men and women grew further apart and took distinctly different paths.

Imagine life in America in the 1830s and '40s. Most people lived on farms. While there were areas of market economy farming like cotton, tobacco, and wheat, the majority of people still grew most of their own food. There were some cities in America, but they were small commercial cities at harbors and along rivers. Men, women, and children had separate and unequal roles in the family, but the family was still an economic unit that worked together. The "little commonwealth" of the family needed each member to survive. It is true that the growing of the major crop was the "man's job," along with his children's labor, while the growing of vegetables, fowl, and livestock; preserving food; and maintaining clothing was the "woman's job." However, no one would survive without both contributions. The garden, the chickens, and the food preservation ensured the family's survival as much, if not more, than the cash crop.

Life in the 1830s and '40s was limited in scope for everyone. Individuals were known by all their neighbors and restricted by the mores of the culture. Men and women were very unequal under law but were more alike in real life. Society was not under great pressure; men and women had a much more even balance of power than they were to have fifty years later. The 1830s saw Watt's improvement of the steam engine which made the

An allegorical sculpture adds the cachet of classical learning to a corner of the parlor at The Abbey in Cape May, New Jersey. (Facing) The architecture is 1860s Gothic Revival; the wallpaper is 1880s Aesthetic Movement; and the furniture is an 1880s Renaissance Revival suite by Herter Brothers. The combination suggests how middle-class, late Victorians would furnish a midcentury cottage in the latest taste. The color scheme is light and clean for the 1880s, but the whole ensemble is convincing for a house at the shore.

railroads and steamboats possible. The completion of the Erie canal in the 1820s opened the near Midwest and the Great Lakes to commerce and settlement. The 1850s saw the discovery of coal and iron together in Pennsylvania, which permitted the cast-iron and steel industries to produce factories in cities and to produce railroads to ship their raw materials and manufactured goods. The Civil War caused the railroads to boom and heavy industry to flourish.

As a result, everything changed in the middle decades of the nineteenth century. America became urbanized. The 1870 census revealed that, for the first time, most Americans lived in cities. In a small town or a farm village, everyone knew each other, and behavior was controlled by the neighbors. In a big city each person was anonymous, and standards for behavior had to be internalized and enforced by the individual. For most of history right and wrong were external rules; now personal morality had to prevail. The ideal of "self-control" for modern people became widespread in the late nineteenth century.

At the same time, the family as an economic unit, a "little commonwealth," disappeared. It was replaced by the modern cash economy where each person is an individual. By the turn of the century in America, most people worked in manufacturing or in offices. The new middle class worked in skyscrapers and took a commuter railroad or "el" (elevated railroad) or trolley to work. "Home" was an apartment or flat or row house. This was a new class of people. They were not the gentry of the eighteenth and early nineteenth century who made their living from owning land that others farmed or from shipping. They were not the "yeoman farmers" who grew their food with their own hands. They were clerks and office workers whose work was not manual and who saw themselves as newly arrived gentry. The Irish potato famine of the 1840s drove millions of immigrants to America,

(Facing) These Rococo Revival chairs by Henry Belter represent the Victorian ideal—modern high technology in historic costume. Belter developed a process for gluing mahogany veneers in a curved mold, creating fancy plywood. He then carved them into caricatures of eighteenth-century, French Rococo chairs, much stronger and more elaborate than the originals.

while revolutions and repressions pushed millions out of Eastern Europe in the 1850s through the '80s. Thus, labor was cheap. Even clerical, white-collar workers could have several servants, either live-in maids or daily cleaning ladies who returned to their (newly invented) tenements at night.

The wives and daughters of the new middle class were not part of the family's economic survival. To confirm their status as the new gentry, office workers' wives cultivated the interests and manners of the gentlewomen of earlier generations. These families had just climbed the slippery slope of social class in one generation. If the woman of the house had to work, the family clearly had not arrived. Instead, the women of the family must cultivate a profound and pure ignorance of how to support themselves. They must learn "not to have a head for figures." They must never do anything that could be remotely interpreted as useful. They must embody high moral standards unsullied by contact with the world and high aesthetic standards to bring beauty and truth to the family.

(Facing) The parlor was the "heart of the home" and the piano the heart of the parlor. This one is a particularly impressive Chickering grand piano in Rococo Revival style. The chairs and walls are equally Louis XV style with the slightly unusual addition of an oriental screen, perhaps because Commodore Perry was a friend of the Howe family, the owners of the house. (Right) Ribbons and thread create a feminine vignette at Rockwood in Delaware. They testify to the exaltation of hand needlework in Victorian times.

What is the result of confining half of the population to their houses with all the necessities of life easily provided for by the new industrial America? The high Victorian parlor. Imagine a woman spending all of her productive years in her parlor and other people's parlors. She is taught that her role is to bring beauty to the home through the nobility of such eighteenth-century crafts as hand needlework. She is forbidden to read serious books or write for fear of taxing her childlike mind. The result would be an explosion of decorative crafts cluttering up every room in the house, especially the parlor.

As an example, take the simple art of flower arranging. Soon everything that could be done with natural flowers had been done. Soon thereafter

the possibilities of dried flowers were exhausted. With cloth and wire and glue, silk flowers can be crafted. With dye and chicken feathers, feather flowers are born. With wire springs and thread, flower petals can be formed and joined together. With shells and glue, shell flowers are made. With the hair of dearly departed loved ones, memorial flower wreaths are fashioned. With gum Arabic or sugar paste or tissue paper or glass beads or foil or mica, flowers can be made and displayed in bouquets under glass domes or in wreaths or as crosses in shadow boxes.

The most popular group of crafts was certainly needlework. Making clothing was far too plebeian and was now accomplished by automatic Singer sewing machines in sweatshops by immigrants. Berlin work was the preferred activity of Victorian ladies. Named for the printed canvasses available from Germany, Berlin work encompassed needlepoint and petit point. It was closely allied to embroidery on prepunched composition board, to regular and counted cross-stitch embroidery, and to crewel work with its wide repertoire of stitches. "Drawn-thread work" could be used to make a fancy border on a simple linen guest towel. Crochet produced a coarse lace while knitting produced many booties and blankets.

Even more characteristic of late Victorian needlework are the bizarre and curious items favored by such popular magazines as *Godey's Lady's Book*. Bits of cloth and cardboard were wrapped in thread and sewn

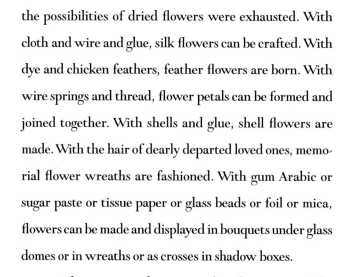

Framed flowers fashioned from human hair are somewhat creepy to us but were a perfect combination of sentimental nostalgia, valued handiwork in the age of the machine, and a taste for prettiness that epitomizes the late nineteenth century. (Facing) Lace, appliqué embroidery, and quilting—all women's crafts— soften a factory-made Eastlake sofa at the Emlen Physick Estate.

together, ornamented with more thread in the form of tassels and pompons, and decorated with glued-on gewgaws to make containers and covers for every imaginable object. Cases and boxes for thread, of course, were needed, for scissors and chalks and eyeglasses and slippers and books and bric-a-brac. If a doily or dainty or antimacassar could support an object or a cozy or cover could surround it or a tidy bow accent it, it was done. No surface was left bare. Every horizontal plane required a cover, every vertical plane a drapery, and every object a receptacle—all made of needlework.

There is a basic difference in the furnishing of parlors in the 1840s,

1860s, and 1880s, apart from the proliferation of handiwork and "art." In the 1840s, the Greek Revival style favored an orderly, symmetrical arrangement of furniture. The furniture was arranged against the walls and upholstered in horsehair or scarlet velvet to match. The effect was very formal with the architecture and furniture perfectly coordinated. This kind of parlor was not for chatty family gatherings and could only be maintained by those who were rich enough to keep one room for visitors.

By the 1850s and '60s, there had been superficial change in style and more basic change in the way the room was used. Furniture was now usually fashioned in a machine-made revival of eighteenth-century French Rococo. It might be called Louis XIV, XV, XVI, or even Marie Antoinette. What is important, however, is that the furniture was now arranged in informal conversational groupings. It was still upholstered "en suite," now most likely in damask, but it was no longer arranged against the wall. Instead, a settee and a few chairs were gathered on the rose-bowered carpet so that ladies could socialize while doing their needlework. The center table under the gaslight was used for reading the paper or books, then cleared for tea with visitors, then cleared again for evening parlor games.

By the 1880s, the parlor had filled up with "art units." The furniture was not likely to be a matched set and was not upholstered to match. The choice and arrangement of objects and furniture in the parlor were primary ways the "lady of the house" could express her artistic sensibilities. By ornamenting and decorating every surface, by arranging easels, lightweight "fairy tables," urns, pedestals, palms, and fans, the mistress

(Facing) Compare this riotous room's bright, lozenge-paneled walls, pastel damask settees and chairs, Aubusson rug, and richly decorated ceiling with the earlier Greek Revival parlor on page sixty to see the whole change wrought by the Industrial Revolution. Sumptuous, palatial, feminine, and French contrast with the simple, sober, and democratic. (Right) Spools of thread reveal what the ladies seated on the damask settee did with their days.

introduced beauty to her family, heightened their aesthetic sensibilities, and fostered a moral and refined atmosphere.

The change in the parlor reflected the change in women's roles. The Greek Revival parlor was a formal room for entertaining. It was spare and uncluttered and not particularly personal. During this period women were restricted by traditional roles but, at least, were part of a cohesive life where their contribution was essential. The Rococo Revival parlor represents a half-way point in the industrialization and urbanization of America. The furniture is now entirely machine-made. The room has become more "feminized" as the roles of men and women have diverged; the workplace has become the man's sphere and the home the woman's. The furniture is arranged in conversational groups as middle-class women are restricted more and more to visiting and handicrafts. By the 1880s, the woman has become a demigoddess of art and morality, and the parlor is her temple. An obsessive and self-conscious decorating and collecting frenzy resulted when women were cut off from participation in the world and made the guardian of the family's aesthetic and moral well-being.

The ivory-colored parlor set in Marie Antoinette style looks as though the ladies went into the next room for tea and didn't return for a hundred years. The upholstery may be shot, but the genuine feeling of the very late nineteenth century, when men and women had hardly anything to do with each other, is almost palpable. (Facing) Parlor games—Parcheesi, chess, charades, etc.—filled the long hours not taken up by visiting and needlework.

Part of personalizing the parlor was filling it with photographs. Through the nineteenth century, tintypes, daguerreotypes, and Eastman's inexpensive box cameras allowed families to memorialize themselves cheaply and often. (Facing) The parlor of the Physick Estate represents the clashing of the two attitudes toward design in the late nineteenth century. Designed in 1879 by Frank Furness, the house originally was radically Aesthetic. After about twenty years, Mrs. Physick couldn't stand it any more and redecorated in "pretty," conventional, French taste.

THE AESTHETIC MOVEMENT

Though the Philistines may jostle, you

will rank as an apostle in the high

aesthetic band,

If you walk down Picadilly with a

poppy or a lily in your medieval

hand.

And everyone will say,

As you walk your flowery way,

"If he's content with a vegetable love

which would certainly not suit me,

Why, what a most particularly pure

young man this pure young man

must be!"

—*Patience*, 1881, William Gilbert

(Facing) The Aesthetic Movement's fondness for Gothic ornament is illustrated by the ceiling, wallpaper, and curtains in the music room at The Abbey. The Renaissance Revival furniture is the posh choice of the 1880s.

THE CONFUSION OF MORAL VALUES and artistic design found expression in the Aesthetic Movement, a credo of the late nineteenth century. At its heart was the belief that good design or beauty is elevating and that bad design or ugliness is corrupting. Followers of the Aesthetic Movement believed that Truth and Beauty were intertwined and that Falsehood and Ugliness were one. Aesthetics, then, had a moral implication, and good proportion, honesty, and harmony with natural laws were as much a characteristic of personal morality as of design.

This movement began in England and was championed by the "Goths," that is, the supporters of the Gothic Revival. In general, they wanted to restore the ritual and mystery of the medieval church and remove the more recent "low church" alterations which bring the congregation and the priest closer together. They came to believe in Gothic as *the* peculiarly English style (despite the Abbé Suger, Notre-Dame de Paris, Saint-Denis, and Chartres).

Aesthetic Movement devotees generally fell into two camps. One camp, led by Ruskin, the greatest art critic of his time, felt that art must be inspired by nature to be true and good, that no creation of compass and rule with mechanical repetition could ever hope to contain the spark of true art.

The most famous practitioner in this branch of the Aesthetic Movement was William Morris, whose plant-design wallpapers and carpets became very popular.

The other camp of aestheticians had a number of famous leaders. They believed that the direct imitation of nature in the applied arts was fakery. They deplored the use of perspective and modeling in wallpapers and carpets and insisted on flat, "conventionalized" forms for flat surfaces. Charles Locke Eastlake was a spokesman for this camp. He wrote *Hints on Household Taste* and made the Aesthetic Movement popular in America. Owen Jones, the chronicler of ornament and cofounder of the South Kensington School (later part of the Victoria and Albert Museum), was a famous champion. The most famous, and later infamous, spokesman for this group of aesthetes was the writer Oscar Wilde. It is through his persecution as a homosexual that the word "aesthetic" has come to have conflicting implications. As a result, the Aesthetic Movement came to be regarded as both a moral crusade and an "immoral effeminate" circle at the same time.

To understand this movement, look at the world against which they were reacting. The middle of the nineteenth century saw the end of hand-

The naturalistic grapevines in this otherwise Rococo gasolier accord with the preference of Ruskin and Morris for realistic forms in the decorative arts. (Facing) Frank Furness's farsighted designs are clear in this Physick Estate bedroom. The overmantel shelf, the footboard of the bed, and the door all feature the repetitive, geometric designs and reeding that would become so popular among people with "advanced" taste over the next decade. The flock of swallows in the stained glass highlights the Japanese influence in the Aesthetic Movement.

crafted home furnishings in America. Just as the Rococo Revival style became popular, it became possible to make everything by the carload. Curved parlor chairs with naturalistically carved roses at the crest became the rage. Wallpapers with roses and ribbons were printed in so many modulated colors that they seemed three-dimensional. Wall-to-wall, Aubusson, patterned carpets had more roses and arabesques. China was transfer-printed with French shepherdesses and more roses. All of this factory-made prettiness in the French taste was cloying to English aesthetic tastes. Badly made furniture and lumpy vases with oddly placed roses made them cringe.

(Facing) This is the parlor in our house, Leith Hall in Cape May. The parlor set, china, glass, and silver are all 1880s Anglo-Japanese, as well as the parasol, the bamboo easel, and the painting displayed on it. We've tried to create a parlor that looks as it might have when the house was newly built. (Right) This vignette illustrates several strains in Victorian décor. The wallpaper is in the French taste, the decorative plate features Queen Victoria, and the bowl is oriental in a frame that revives the Rococo. None of these juxtapositions would have disturbed an eclectic Victorian.

Where did the Victorians turn to get away from the industrial Rococo, from trompe l'oeil and cute decorations? They turned to several sources: the East (specifically Japan), the Middle East (specifically Turkey), and their own medieval past. These seemingly unrelated traditions all seemed of a piece to Aesthetic Movement followers. They all represented pre-industrial societies. They didn't use perspective. And, best of all, they weren't French. Commodore Perry had opened Japan to Western commerce in the mid-nineteenth century. By the time of the Philadelphia Exposition of 1876, Americans were curious about this exotic culture. The spectacular Japanese pavilion launched a Japanese craze. When we look at Japanese design with modern eyes, we see what modern architects saw—spare, empty rooms with tatami mats and shoji screens, restrained interiors with no superfluous decoration. Victorians, however, saw the two-dimensional patterns of Japanese cottons, the sumptuous fabrics of kimonos, a whole repertoire of geometric and natural motifs such as cranes, bamboo, swallows, and plum blossoms. They saw the complexity and seeming randomness of asymmetrical paintings, fans, and screens.

Olana is perhaps the greatest exotic revival building in the United States. The home of Frederick Church, the Hudson River school painter, it goes further in the picturesque, romantic, Moorish direction than any house we know.

The Turkish side of the Aesthetic Movement appealed to many middle-class homeowners. A Turkish corner in the parlor brought the atmosphere of the decadent East into the most proper home. Turkey, after all, was constantly in the newspapers as the Ottoman Empire gradually declined. To the Victorians anything Middle Eastern was Turkish, and authenticity was of very little concern. Bedspreads imported from India, big pillows, hookahs, and tassels created a suitably sexy lounging area. Egyptian ornament appealed to the side of the Aesthetic Movement that favored conventionalized plant motifs. Islamic interlace was flat and geometric, and Persian rugs were ideal. Because we have been putting oriental carpets on floors ever since the late nineteenth century, they have lost all their shock value for us. To people accustomed to flowery, wall-to-wall carpet, as the homeowners of the 1870s were, the sight of several unmatched Persian carpets on a bare floor brought to mind the bazaars of Marakesh or Casablanca, the decadent harems and drug traffic of North Africa. Most of us also

miss the implications of a sofa, a club chair, or an ottoman. To late Victorians, all fully upholstered, inner-spring seat furniture was new. It had just been invented, and it was all considered Turkish. Sofa and divan are both Arab words, and ottoman, of course, refers to the Ottoman Empire of Turkey. This furniture was decadent not only because it was Middle Eastern but also because it encourages lounging. This was the first furniture that didn't require the sitter to sit up like a lady or a gentleman; the sitter could lean back like a pasha. Imagine how sexy that was to a Victorian.

(Facing) This room at Olana features Frederick Church's paintings in the exotic setting of an Islamic fireplace, interlace patterned door-surrounds and borders, as well as a "Turkish" club chair. Seldom have the exterior and interior of a house been so cohesive. (Right) Victorian porch posts at Olana ought to be overlooking the Nile rather than the Hudson.

The medieval element of the Aesthetic Movement was very strong. The straightforward Gothic Revival is covered in the styles chapter, but the Aesthetic Movement considered its own geometric, repetitive designs to be Modern Gothic. Eastlake's furniture and Christopher Dresser's futuristic wallpapers and pottery were both called Modern Gothic at the time. These designers relied on flattened, conventionalized plant forms that look heraldic. Flowers were arranged as though on a gothic tapestry. Diaper patterns were borrowed from wall paintings of the Middle Ages. What they meant by Modern Gothic was the lack of perspective and modeling which they borrowed from pre-Renaissance decorative painting. This medieval side was a nostalgic look at a romanticized past, a reaction against the growing dominance of the machine, and a longing for the simple life that handmade objects represented.

The Aesthetic Movement was always a minority movement but, by tying the decoration of one's parlor to one's moral character, it heightened the importance of the woman's role in the home and supported the image of the woman as the caretaker of moral values for the family.

(Facing) The smoking corner shows how much Victorians thought style should be appropriate to use. Tobacco was Turkish, so smoking rooms featured Islamic interlace on the walls, built-in seating in the manner of a pasha's court, and, of course, ottomans. (Right) This ceiling resembles nothing so much as the ceiling of the ground floor at the Sainte Chapelle in Paris. Sometimes the Gothic Revival came remarkably close to the Gothic, especially in the hands of Alexander Jackson Davis in his later years.

STYLES

(Page 52-53)
All the earmarks of the Italianate style— the heavy horizontal emphasis, overhanging cornice, big brackets, square massing, a cupola, and arched windows—are present in this beautiful example of Tuscan villa style. (Facing) The freedom to create new forms in the Cottage Gothic style is evident; here a three-part window, a Renaissance motif associated with Palladio, has been Gothicized with a pointed arch and label lintels. (Right) The cyma curve of the arm of this American Empire (Greek Revival) settee would make Sophocles feel right at home, while the eagle-winged foot reminds us that this was actually Jacksonian America.

OFTEN WHEN A MODERN PERSON looks at nineteenth-century architecture, it seems like a confusing babble of warring styles. The "modern" movement in architecture, also known as the "International Style," fostered this view of the nineteenth century by condemning all "historical" styles and ornament. The modernists of the twentieth century disdained all applied decoration. They condemned it as shallow, fake, and contrary to good principles of proportion, honesty of materials and structure, and creative shaping of space, all of which were held to be the proper measures of architecture. In doing this, the modernists were guilty of a present-mindedness and reductionism that caused them to condemn an entire century without bothering to understand it.

Historical styles had a lot of content to nineteenth-century people. In this chapter, we'll look at three styles out of many: the Greek Revival, the Gothic Revival, and the Italianate.

GREEK REVIVAL

Ancient sculpture is the true school of modesty. But where the Greeks had modesty, we have cant; where they had patriotism, we have cant; where they had anything that exalts, delights, or adorns humanity, we have nothing but cant, cant, cant.

—*Crotchet Castle*, 1831, Thomas Love Peacock

THE GREEK REVIVAL IN AMERICA should be seen in the context of a growing nationalism, a widening of democracy, and a provincial boosterism that trumpeted America as profoundly different from anywhere else on earth. In the eighteenth century, America built in a colonial version of prevailing British styles. The grandest houses in America were the equivalent of very small-scale merchants' town houses in England. We had no mansions comparable to the great country houses of England. In style as well as scale, our houses were modest. They were usually designed in a slightly mixed-up version of the late Baroque that is generally known as Georgian.

It took ages for the English to wake up to the Renaissance. So, classical architecture came to England very late after the Baroque had modified the Renaissance in Italy. During the seventeenth and eighteenth centuries, it finally came to root itself in Britain. By the very late eighteenth century, a new, refined classicism swept both England and the United States. Called Adamesque in England and Federal in the United States, it harked

(Facing) The giant columns and full-length veranda of this private home in Saratoga Springs, New York, are most characteristic of late Greek Revival hotels. (Right) The shadows of ironwork on these Doric bases reveal the combination of exquisite refinement and monumentality characteristic of the best Greek Revival architecture.

back to Roman models to create a much more archaeologically correct classicism. After all, it had been hundreds of years since Renaissance Italy first revived Roman styles of building. These styles had been modified by time and travel and had become part of European culture.

When Herculaneum and Pompeii were discovered and their style widely disseminated by late eighteenth-century French steel engravings, real classical style came as quite a shock. Architects realized how far

classicism had come from its Greco-Roman roots, and, on the whole, they liked the originals better. Architects like the Adam brothers in England adopted the new slim and elegant classicism, and it came to be used in the United States as well. In England, Adamesque ornament had very little ideological content. It was just decorative. In the United States, after the Revolution, it came to represent republican government. The new capital at Washington was filled with Federal-style buildings in direct reference to republican Rome. The Roman classical style was adopted by the revolutionaries in France as well, to symbolize the break with the old monarchy. In time the new Roman style was adopted by Napoléon and made showier and more bombastic to represent the Roman Empire in its new incarnation under the Emperor Napoléon.

This was the background, then, in the 1830s. Americans were well acquainted with classicism and associated Roman classicism with the generation of the founding fathers. The nation was turning away from the Eastern seaboard and focusing on the trans-Appalachian West. In 1825, the Erie Canal was opened, encouraging commerce in the West. In 1807, Robert Fulton had demonstrated his steamboat, and by the 1830s dozens of steamboats plied the Hudson. In 1830, Peter Cooper displayed his midget engine, the Tom Thumb, and began a transportation revolution in railroads. In 1827, Americans rose up and elected Andrew Jackson president and threw out the last vestige of the Founding Fathers in the person of John Quincy Adams. Americans believed the age of Jackson to be the era of the common man, and the 1830s to be an American social revolution. It is no wonder that the elegance and refinement of the Federal style now seemed wrong.

The Greek Revival style in America pervaded the smallest details of everyday life. Women wore light muslin dresses with Empire waists and no crinolines. They put their hair up in Greek style. Houses and public

(Facing) Note that the dressing table legs are Greek lyres, and the mirror supports are volutes. This is how a successful merchant, Seabury Treadwell, could show his commitment to democracy in New York City in 1832.

buildings were erected as little temples in small frontier towns in western New York and Ohio and Georgia. The towns themselves were named Athens, Syracuse, Troy, and Rome. A lamp to read by, a fork to eat with, a chair to sit on were all Greek inspired.

Why Greek? Because the Greeks invented democracy. However, in classical times, democracy meant mob-rule, and a republic meant rule by the people. It didn't matter that only a small proportion of ancient Greeks actually got to participate in government. It was only during the Enlightenment that the attitude toward the common man changed from "the mob" to the "noble savage," and democracy became desirable. To Americans, however, democracy was a Greek concept and the rule of the common man was democracy.

The Greek Revival in interiors is usually called American Empire, and it was a style admirably suited to the new realities of American life.

A Greek honeysuckle or anthemion decorates the Taylor Grady house mantle. Classical ornaments such as these turned up in ironwork, fabric, and plaster during the Greek Revival period.

Empire furniture is usually made of mahogany veneer sheathing substantial monumental shapes. Carving, which had been such a prominent feature of the Federal style, practically disappeared. The furniture achieved its effect by the beauty of its surfaces and the drama of its silhouette. A modern viewer might not realize that it is the first mass-produced, machine-made furniture in America. New steam and water-powered sawmills could cut Honduras mahogany into inexpensive veneers. New, machine-tooled casters and nuts and bolts joined bed parts into a whole. New transportation opened larger markets and made large-scale furniture factories profitable.

The simplicity of American Empire furniture appealed to the common man of Jacksonian America. The low price appealed to the common man as well. Americans saw themselves as noble, honest democrats, founding a new egalitarian system in the wilderness. What better furnishings could there be than simple, sturdy, egalitarian Greek? This feeling was very profound, but fleeting. The country changed so quickly between the 1830s and 1850s that new needs had to be met by a new architecture and a new furniture style.

GOTHIC REVIVAL

One must have taste to be sensible of the beauties of Grecian architecture; one only wants passions to feel Gothic.

—Horace Walpole (1717-97)

(Facing) Lyndhurst began as an early nineteenth-century "cottage Gothic" house by Alexander Jackson Davis. He enlarged it twice over his long career and made it one of the most beautiful and complex Gothic style houses in the country. Andrew Jackson Downing published illustrations of the house and kept Davis's style current long after the more archeological High Victorian Gothic and the freer Modern Gothic were in vogue.

BY THE 1850S, AMERICANS HAD BECOME nervous and disoriented by the Industrial Revolution. The advances of the 1830s and 1840s were successful. The steam engine, canal building, railroads, trolleys, steamboats, urbanization, and immigration had transformed everyday life. More and more, Americans worked in factories and lived in cities. More and more, Americans left their families and looked for work on their own. More and more, everything around them was unfamiliar, machine-made, and unpredictable. The increasing pace of change caused a backlash, a "future shock" reaction. A conservative longing for the good old days of yeoman farmers, traditional rural family life, and old-time religion found its expression in the Gothic Revival.

The anonymity of city life, the insecurity of working in a market economy, and the disruption of the traditional social hierarchy made Americans profoundly uneasy and supported our first conservative movement. England had gone through the same experiences about fifty years earlier and had reacted in the same way. Our Gothic Revival was derived from their Gothic Revival.

Early in the nineteenth century, England was searching for a national style. Deeply conservative, the English saw their freedoms as deriving from an endless succession of small precedents, stretching back to the Middle Ages. The English yeoman virtues of modesty, stability, and honesty were contrasted with the revolutionary, high-flown philosophical

and unstable traits of the French. Under Napoléon, the French had adopted Imperial Rome as their national model and were busily demolishing medieval monasteries like Cluny. So the English came to think of Gothic as their own national style.

Once Gothic is thought of as English, all sorts of characteristics fit in. Gothic is quirky and disorderly. The English prize eccentricity and built their legal system on an endlessly complex structure of precedents. The French, on the other hand, were basing their law on rigorously applied philosophical principles and rigidly codified them in the Code Napoléon. The Gothic style is pragmatic and can accommodate mismatched uses and spaces. The English tradition was pragmatic and accommodated conflicts for a thousand years without revolution and bloodshed (Cromwell always excepted). The French, on the other hand, killed their king and then killed each other over very small differences during the revolution.

(Facing) Lyndhurst proved the assertion by Davis and Downing that Gothic is a more practical style for country houses than Greek because it easily lends itself to additions and alterations. (Right) The medieval air of this bay at the Henry Bowen House brings the romantic light of olde England to Woodstock, Connecticut.

It is no wonder, then, that the English looked to honest medieval architecture and honest medieval workmanship. The buildings were naked expressions of their structure with the skeleton of flying buttresses and ribbed vaulting exposed. The furniture kept the "unvarnished truth" of oak joinery, fresh from the chisel. Many supporters of the Gothic Revival were also part of a conservative movement in the Anglican Church. Organizations such as the Cambridge Camden Society and the Oxford Group sought to rid Anglican churches of their post-medieval alterations and to restore them to their "gothic purity." They also sought to rid the Church of

England of its low-church Protestant tradition and to emphasize its catholic (just not *Roman* Catholic) apostolic roots. Thus, the Gothic Revival became associated with a "conservative," religious sentiment pushing Anglicanism toward medieval, ritualistic, high doctrine and away from low-church Methodism.

The Oxford Group and the Cambridge Camden Society went around England drawing parish churches and urging parishes to preserve them.

Where changes in worship had been reflected in physical changes in the church, these enthusiasts pushed for restoration. They preferred ritual and mystery with a distant priesthood to accessibility and clarity with a pastoral minister. In America, the Gothic Revival is first associated with Episcopal churches. After a time, this specific association broadened into a general romantic view of medieval virtues like simplicity, modesty, and naturalness.

An author and landscape architect named Andrew Jackson Downing did more than anyone else to popularize the gothic cottage in America. Along with architect Alexander Jackson Davis, he designed modest country houses in an irregular cottage style only vaguely gothic. We should remember, however, that after two hundred years of classicism, any building that was asymmetrical and picturesque looked very gothic indeed. Downing declared that Davis's houses were more "natural" than Greek Revival temples (though what's natural about a building is hard to say). He recommended "natural" colors like sand, fawn, and stone.

He described them as "country houses" to increase the appeal of nature, though they were most often built in the suburbs. In short, Downing's

A Gothic patterned ceiling carries the texture of the decoration over every surface. (Facing) Gothic Revival furniture was patterned after Gothic buildings, not medieval furniture, as evidenced by this lovely ecclesiastical-looking chair. It could easily be a window in a cathedral. The all-over texture of the wallcovering dates it as a late nineteenth-century product.

cottages appealed to those values Americans were looking for and had just lost: rural village life and traditional religion. New technology helped Americans conquer the trans-Appalachian West, move into cities, and create an industrial revolution. Naturally, they missed being English yeoman farmers.

As the nineteenth century progressed, the Industrial Revolution built up a head of steam and took off. With the demand for war matériel

caused by the Civil War and post-war rebuilding in the North, the tendencies of the 1850s were continued. Americans became more urban, industrial, atomized, anonymous, and immigrant. Of course, the reaction continued, too. The Cottage Gothic of the 1840s and '50s became the High Victorian Gothic of the 1860s and '70s. The more archaeologically correct High Victorian Gothic gave way to the Aesthetic Movement (called Modern Gothic in its day). The Aesthetic Movement succumbed to the Queen Anne style, which was the culmination and last gasp of the cozy, picturesque, medieval, country-house movement that Downing began fifty years before. All of these styles have physical traits in common: the irregular massing, the picturesque silhouette, the asymmetrical facade. But, more important, they all have a message in common: the home as an escape from urban stress, the free-standing house in its own plot of land to confirm the stability of property, and the Englishness of the American heritage to balance the tidal wave of immigrants reaching the United States' shores.

(Facing) In the Victorian scheme of gender-typing rooms, the library was male. This Gothic library shows the dark, oaken, monastic ideal for study. (Right) The romantic massing and irregularity of the Gothic Revival not only provided for dark monastic spaces, but also for light-filled halls illuminated by window walls of mullioned glass. Unlike more classical styles, windows could be designed for the shape and size that were wanted on the inside rather than needed on the façade.

ITALIANATE

Report of fashions in proud Italy,

Whose manners still our tardy apish

nation

Limps after in base imitation.

—*King Richard II*, William Shakespeare

THE ITALIANATE STYLE REPRESENTS the other side of Americans' reaction to the Industrial Revolution. The existence of a nostalgic reaction against the Industrial Revolution shouldn't blind us to the fact that most people believed that there was no time and no place better in which to live. Americans believed in progress. They believed that "every day in every way things were getting better and better." They knew that they had more opportunity for education, for acquaintance with fine arts, music, and drama, and for leisure and luxury.

They agreed with Dr. Samuel Johnson, who dismissed country village living as "the idiocy of rural life." Most Americans in the mid-nineteenth century knew that civilization lay in the city. In examining the institutions of "high culture," it is astonishing how many of them were founded in the late nineteenth century. Almost all academic fields were codified in the 1880s. Modern history, psychology, and the natural sciences date from the 1880s. The Metropolitan Opera and the Metropolitan Museum of Art in New York, along with many symphonies and ballets, date from the late nineteenth century. By contrast, a museum in the early- to mid-nineteenth century was as likely to be a sideshow or a cabinet of curiosities like Barnum's Museum.

However, by the late nineteenth century, museums such as the

(Facing) Italianate public buildings displayed many of the same features as homes—heavy cornices with brackets, segmental arches, and horizontal emphasis. While most detached houses were based on irregular "villa" prototypes, city buildings like this one were based on the three-part division of a "palazzo"—base, middle, and cornice.

American Museum of Natural History, the Smithsonian Institution, and the Metropolitan Museum of Art were underway. The modern university was developed in Germany, also in the 1880s. The old colleges and universities in the United States had been founded as seminaries in the seventeenth and eighteenth centuries. At the end of the nineteenth century, they changed their focus and adopted the new German standards of scholarship. Many universities expanded and many new schools were founded in the Midwest.

Improved printing technology after the Civil War made inexpensive magazines, newspapers, and dime novels everyday fare for the common man.

As a result of this explosion of knowledge and the arts, many people were exposed to information their parents couldn't have dreamed of. A successful businessman in the late-nineteenth century tried to be familiar with the most respected artists of the Renaissance. An industrial or commercial tycoon might take the "grand tour" as a young man, visiting Italy, Greece, France, and England, seeing the great works of art in the context of their native architecture. Even a regular white-collar worker might have seen a Raphael or a Tintoretto in a local museum and might own a chromolithograph or photograph of fine art framed on his wall.

How did these substantial burghers see themselves and their homes? What kind of house would express this self-satisfaction with civilized "modern" life? Something Renaissance. Most big city houses were Italianate row houses. Taking their general organization from Italian city houses called palazzi, the row houses consisted of a rusticated base, a

(Left and facing) The Mainstay Inn was originally Jackson's Clubhouse, a gentlemen's gambling house. It features Italianate ornament and massing, but the details are so original as to have left their classical roots behind.

smooth middle with classical windows, and a bracketed cornice. While the Italian Renaissance palazzo had been many bays wide, the middle-class row house was usually restricted to three and was much taller than wide. Whole blocks of palazzo-like facades were built by real-estate developers, however, and together they created a suitably horizontal impression. Renaissance palazzi were also the model for most civic and arts-related buildings, for clubhouses, schools, and even for cast-iron factories and warehouses.

In less dense towns and in new suburbs where free-standing buildings were economically feasible, the Italian Renaissance villa was often the model. During the nineteenth century, the English and Americans called all free-standing, suburban houses villas. The English still do. In those days, many suburban houses were villas in more than name. Low pitched roofs, cupolas, heavy bracketed cornices, loggias, belvederes, and pergolas were features of many suburban villas.

(Facing) The segmental arch, an arch composed of less than half of a circle, is the signature of the Italianate style. Here a prosperous Italianate interior bespeaks the calm poise that follows from a knowledge of Renaissance culture. (Right) This arcade supporting a classical cornice is in the Park-McCullough House in North Bennington, Vermont, as is the previous picture, but the imagery is of a baldachino at the Vatican or a reception room in Florence.

Inside the Italianate house, the most ambitious displayed classical and Renaissance statuary, sometimes made of marble or bronze, but usually plaster or cast-iron. The parlor furniture was likeliest to be French Rococo Revival because the parlor was considered to be a "woman's room." The strictly divided gender roles of the time were applied to the various rooms in the house. The dining room and the library were thought of as man's territory, and here one might properly place "Renaissance" furniture. This furniture had almost no relationship to that found in the Italian Renaissance. It

simply identified any furniture with classical ornament such as modillions or grotesques and a pronounced horizontal cornice. The more it looked like an Italianate house, the more it was Renaissance furniture.

The monumentalism of Italianate furniture continued through the 1850s and '60s, faded somewhat in the Aesthetic Movement of the 1870s and mid '80s, and was reincarnated in the 1880s and '90s as Renaissance Revival. By the 1880s, two factors made Aesthetic Movement furniture unpopular with a growing sector of the population. Aesthetic Movement decoration was too restrained, and furniture factories had cheapened its appeal by churning out inexpensive bedroom "suites." This left the wealthier middle-class homeowner with no style of his own. In the mid-1880s, Aesthetic Movement shapes were ornamented with cartouches bearing classical women's faces and topped by heavy cornices to make them Italianate. Eastlake furniture thus continued as working-class, and the new Renaissance Revival became the high-class version.

This ceiling corner composed of Renaissance rinceaux displays the lightness and frothiness that identify it as French, and as Rococo. (Facing) In this Charleston single house, the organization of the Italianate row house is still there—base, middle, and cornice; however, the details have changed. By the 1870s and '80s, the foliate brackets have become geometric in response to Eastlake's influence, and the style is Aesthetic Movement, sometimes called Neo-Grec.

HOW THE WEST WAS WON

The blessings of our art should be diffused through the west, and that, improvements in shaving and hairdressing, should go hand in hand with the progress of high steam and bank paper.

—1819, Edward F. Pratt, Philadelphia barber

(Pages 78-79) The 1844 Delameter House was designed by Alexander Jackson Davis and publicized by Andrew Jackson Downing. Downing's books spread the message of the Gothic Revival across the United States. His picturesque cottages were copied throughout the frontier. (Facing) Here in Athens, Georgia, this Greek colonnade shows what settlers valued when the frontier was just across the Appalachians. This is called the House of the President of the University of Georgia and was built at the very end of the Greek Revival era (1857-58).

HOW DID THE VICTORIAN HOUSE come to be where it is—in the particular part of town where it is located, or in the part of the country where it was built? In the eighteenth century, almost everyone got around on foot. While most people lived in the country, town-dwellers concentrated at the mouths of rivers and good natural harbors. Cities were very dense and very small because everyone walked everywhere. Residential, commercial, and industrial areas didn't separate until transportation improved.

In the 1830s, the horse streetcar allowed people to live somewhere other than where they worked. This enabled exclusively residential neighborhoods to develop for the first time. In big cities, Greek Revival row houses and, in less dense towns, Greek Revival "villas" were built for thriving merchants. This is also the period of the steam engine. The improvements in steamboats and the digging of canals opened the trans-Appalachian West to trade with Eastern cities. That is why there are so many Greek Revival houses in Ohio, West Virginia, western New York state, Kentucky, northern Georgia, and Tennessee. Even the city names attest to America's fascination with the classics—Athens in Tennessee and Georgia; Troy in Ohio and New York; Rome in Georgia and New York; Attica and Utica in

Ohio and New York, with another Attica in Indiana; Greece, Elmira, and Syracuse in New York; Xenia and Philo in Ohio; Apollo and Arcadia in Pennsylvania.

In 1893, Frederick Jackson Turner gave an address looking for an answer to the question "What makes Americans different?" Why are Americans democratic, proud rather than servile, self-sufficient, and independent? His answer was "The Frontier." Americans, when they felt constrained by the rules of Eastern cities, hitched up the wagons and headed West. The West was the home of the loner—the pioneer family setting off to farm the trackless waste, unfettered by Eastern businessmen, city slickers, and class distinctions. Turner mourned the closing of the Frontier in the 1890s and grieved for the passing away of the hardy frontiersman. His view of the settling of the West worked its way down to high school textbooks and many a WPA mural in post offices and public schools across America. The Frontier thesis provided John Wayne with a career. It provided us with a patriotic view of American history.

The only problem is, it wasn't true. The West was actually settled first by cities. In the early nineteenth century, the West was the Ohio territory. Cities such as Cincinnati, Pittsburgh, St. Louis, Louisville, and Lexington preceded the settlement of the surrounding farmland. In *The Urban Frontier*, Richard Wade shows that, far from setting off into the wilderness to farm, settlers tried to move near an existing city. Only when trade was regular and dependable did farmers till adjacent lands and send their crops to market. American farming was commercial, not subsistence, farming, and, until there was a way to get the crop to market, there was little point to raising tons of corn and wheat. Wade quotes a St. Louis editor in 1820, "Cities have arisen in the very wilderness, . . . and form in their respective states the *foci* of art and science, of wealth and information."

(Facing) At the Taylor-Grady House, this Greek Revival dining room is filled with the democratic design that was promulgated by pattern books throughout the trans-Appalachian West. The simple chairs and walls were thought to be appropriate to the yeoman farmer of Jacksonian America.

As for leaving behind the class distinctions of the East, an 1826 Directory proclaimed, "We have our castes of society, graduated and divided with as much regard to rank and dignity as the most scrupulous Hindus maintain." This first American Frontier, across the Alleghenies, depended upon river commerce for its lifeblood. The steamboat reinforced the commercial character of these cities and allowed them to boom.

The second wave of western settlement in the latter half of the nineteenth century was also a product of the steam engine, this time in the form of the railroad. The settling of the Great Plains is a direct result of the building of the railroads, and the railroads came about through the combination of big-city money and government action. Railroads were subsidized by cities eager to be stopping places for western travelers. Companies got enormous real-estate incentives to tempt them to build. The New York and Oswego Midland Railroad (1873) actually zigzags across New York state from municipal bribe to municipal bribe. This system was so pervasive that the line never actually touches a major city because they wouldn't pay up. In 1860, Cincinnati built a railroad southward. In 1861, St. Louis contributed six million dollars for a competing line.

Though the railroad created the Midwest, it was not really intentional. Daniel Boorstin, in *The Americans*, comments, "The Union Pacific Railway Charter in 1862 was meant less to provide a link to the plains then to assure a speedy bridge across them … connecting settlers in the Mississippi Valley with those on the Pacific Coast." Small railroads opened up the territory in between and provided access to markets and transportation for settlement. Boorstin states, "The American railroad, like the booster hotel and the community newspaper of the upstart city, was often built in the hope that the railroad itself would help call into being the population which by serving it would prosper."

(Facing) The elegant proportions of these Greek Revival chairs and the Greek Revival woodwork show the depth of the style in American culture, whether in New York City, in Charleston, or in Athens, Georgia.

Another myth about the independent pioneers is their hostility to government telling them what to do. In fact, when the pioneer got off the train in the West, the one thing he wanted most was more government. The myth of the pioneer settlement with no land-use law is a creation of conservative myth. Although individuals had many more opportunities to acquire land, they needed the government to legitimize their claims to owning it. Without this support, their possession of the land was insecure.

The railroads determined the location of Victorian houses in the West. The coast and the Mississippi Valley came first. San Francisco in California and other mining towns such as Silver Springs and Leadville in Colorado were the urban pioneers of the 1850s and '60s. Then came the myriad, railroad station, real-estate promotion towns that often fizzled and occasionally boomed. The hub of the railroad web that covered the Midwest was Chicago. It grew at the point where the Chicago River emptied into Lake Michigan, on low-lying, swampy ground. That may be the origin of its Native American name, thought to mean "big smell" or "big onion." In 1871, the Great Fire leveled the city and, as it was rebuilt, the Panic of 1873 wiped it out financially. Chicago's location at the center of the railroads, however, fated it to rise again.

What did the Victorian houses of the Midwest look like? How were they different from their Eastern and Pacific counterparts? The answer is they weren't. And the reason they weren't different is that they weren't made locally. By the time the railroads linked the Midwest to the cities of the East, houses were commercial products. The same brackets, balusters, spindles and mantles could be ordered from a millwork catalogue from a company in Chicago, Kansas, or New York. On the Great Plains where there wasn't a tree to be found for hundreds of miles, every stick had to be brought in by train. So, of course, there was no indigenous folk architecture.

(Facing) The Edmonston-Alston House was built in 1828 by a Scottish businessman. The panic of 1837 forced Edmonston to sell the house to Charles Alston. The Greek Revival porticos were probably added by the next owner in 1838. The house has remained virtually unchanged since then and is still lived in by the family.

In fact, the very first houses were "soddies"—houses built of turf blocks by the first settlers or by isolated farmers. Impossible to keep clean and home to insects and snakes galore, the "soddies" were a temporary adaptation to fiercely difficult conditions. As soon as they could, midwestern settlers built the same Stick-Style, Italianate, and Queen Anne houses they had known back east.

By the early twentieth century, Sears, Roebuck and Company, the merchandising giant of Chicago, offered entire houses as kits. Every piece was precut, with barrels of nails and bundles of shingles, ready

for assembly like a giant Tinkertoy. Kit houses were not the poor sister of custom-built houses. In fact, they were much better made. If Sears had cut all the pieces of a house out of average lumber, packed them up, and loaded them into a sidecar, the pieces would have warped, bowed, and checked so much by the time they reached the customer that the house couldn't be put together. In a custom-built house, each piece is cut to fit the previous one and nailed in place immediately. Sears discovered that it needed to use extra-dry, straight-grained lumber to make the whole idea work. In terms of style, Sears houses were no different than the houses of the Eastern seaboard. The inexpensive models may be a little plainer, but the top of the line, eclectic numbers are as decorated as any.

Cast-iron building parts enabled everything from fence posts to department stores to be factory-made and erected anywhere.

Jigsaw decoration or "gingerbread" was ordered from catalogues and enabled styles to move with lightning speed from coast to coast.

Another Midwestern staple was the pattern-book house. Predesigned houses, with plans, elevations, and sections, were available by mail everywhere in the country. The idea goes back to the Renaissance with the illustrations for the many editions of Palladio's *Four Books of Architecture* serving as the model for many a classical villa. In the United States and Canada, however, "builders' companions" by authors like Batty Langley, Asher Benjamin, and Minard Lafever popularized the new Greek Revival style and facilitated its rapid spread through the trans-Appalachian West. The Gothic Revival style, the romantic alternative to classical Greek, was also spread through the new West by publications, especially Andrew Jackson Downing's *Victorian Cottage Residences.*

The style of a Victorian house, then, does not depend much upon location. By the late nineteenth century, the style of a house might depend upon fashion or taste or the wealth of the owner, but the United States, by that time, covered the continent. We had a national economy and a nationwide culture. Houses carried similar messages across the country.

THE BEDROOM

IN THE EARLY NINETEENTH CENTURY, there was no standard size for beds, and beds might be found in any room in the house. Often they were short and very wide as most people slept almost sitting up, and children and guests were bedded in with mother and father.

Beds were standard size by the late nineteenth century: single, three-quarters, and full. In the Wild West, a traveler might pay a fee to share a bed, but to a middle-class couple this would have been unthinkable. Privacy and delicacy were raised to such a fever pitch that the bedroom became strictly off-limits to guests. Middle-class sensibilities even prescribed that bedrooms and public rooms must always be on separate floors so that there should be no promiscuous mixing of the public and private spheres. It was just this feeling that made middle-class people reluctant to live in apartment buildings with bedrooms and parlors adjoining. Most important, the bedroom was the scene of many of the major passages of life: birth, marriage, and death. Before people visited hospitals, the bedroom was their entrance and exit from the world.

SEX AND SIN

MOST AMERICANS BELIEVE that the dissolution of the traditional family, the obsession with sex, and the interference of politics in private life are modern problems—they're not. They started in the last quarter of the nineteenth century.

(Pages 90-91) This monumental bedroom reveals several design strains of the 1890s. The chairs in the foreground are Chippendale, showing the new interest in eighteenth-century American design inherent in the Colonial Revival style. The bed is Renaissance, the mirror is French, and the hearth rug is oriental. (Facing) This vignette of a bedside shows the eclecticism of the very late nineteenth century. The floral theme attractively unites the foliate headboard, Colonial Revival wallpaper, and even the globe of the kerosene lamp.

In the early 1800s, most Americans were rural. Most Americans were perfectly aware of sex and reproduction from childhood, as every farm child must be. Sex was assumed to be for reproduction and was not particularly a subject of great attention. Teenagers married young so premarital sex did not develop into a social question. Even then, betrothed or engaged couples frequently engaged in sex, as up to 30 percent of first children were conceived before marriage. However, the inception of a first child didn't create insurmountable obstacles because the couple lived in a village with relatives, ministers, and neighbors all exerting social pressure. There was enough land for a young couple to get married and clear another farm.

Prostitution was rare in early America. It may be "the oldest profession," but there weren't many unsupervised men around in most places. Large, commercial cities such as New York, Philadelphia, and Boston

certainly contained prostitutes on the waterfront. Mining towns and army camps did, too. But, on the whole, most men were born, lived, and died among their families and neighbors and never visited a large city. Most women had roles in their families and communities and were not driven to desperate measures to survive. Life for women may have been restricting and unequal, but it was part of a cohesive whole in which people were not thought of as individuals, but as family members.

By the late nineteenth century, all that had changed. The economic unit of the farm family was replaced by the individual worker as employee. Men and women left their homes and went off alone to find a job in the big

(Left and facing) These views of a bedroom at the Physick Estate are more feminine than most. Dr. Physick was a bachelor who lived with his mother and her sister. The light approach to the interior also reflects the seaside location of the house. The bed was designed by Frank Furness, the architect who built the house.

city. Most young people lived in boarding houses, rooming houses, or tenements, with no one to know or care what they did. Most women faced bleak job prospects with no support from family or neighbors. As a result, prostitution boomed. In the late nineteenth century, city guidebooks for "gentlemen" openly listed whorehouses as attractions. City women, deprived of the protection of traditional life and denied any other way to make a living, often turned to prostitution as a necessity.

Pornography, like prostitution, may be as old as mankind, but wasn't common in early America. Several transformations in everyday life in the late nineteenth century contributed to its popularity. The development of inexpensive photography was immediately turned to titillation in the form of naughty pictures. Electricity and cheap printing, along with wood-pulp paper, made dime novels and dirty books widely available. The anonymity of big city life provided a ready market.

Middle-class women were horrified by the pornography and prostitution explosion. They saw their own lives being restricted by the increasing narrowness of Victorian gender roles. Once, middle-class women were an integral part of the "little commonwealth" of the farm family, now they were forbidden to work and led a marginal existence. The last bastion of women's authority was the home, and the enemy was the saloon and the whorehouse. It is no wonder that the twin crusades of temperance and antivice were joined and backed up by Protestant evangelism and the fledgling medical profession. The greatest institution of this "social purity" movement was the Women's Christian Temperance Union, and the greatest spokesman was Anthony Comstock.

Earlier in the nineteenth century, the double-standard for men and women was universally accepted. Women were expected to be chaste and men were not. The "social purity" movement sought to replace it with the

(Facing) Here the lady of the house can perform her toilette in classical splendor. The chair features Greek lyre back supports, the mirror has Italian Renaissance consoles, and the vanity sits on Louis XVI legs. Taken all together the style is mid-nineteenth century Italian Renaissance.

"single standard" of chastity before marriage and fidelity afterward for both men and women. To achieve that goal, they mobilized whatever forces they could.

Early in the nineteenth century, prostitutes were considered an evil force in the world, and most authority was from local clergy. By the late nineteenth century, prostitutes were generally described as victims, and most authority was from doctors. The temperance and antivice crusades were largely women's movements and sometimes contained the seeds of other feminist issues. Women social workers and activists suggested that if poor women had equal pay for equal work they would not need to turn to prostitution. In the 1870s and '80s, the Women's Christian Temperance Union declared that the chief cause of fallen women was fallen men.

In 1885, they changed the name of the Committee for Work with Fallen Women to the Social Purity Division, preaching the "white life for two." Leaders of the movement, Susan B. Anthony and Elizabeth Cady Stanton, even went so far as to equate prostitution with marriage, each being an exchange of sex for economic security.

The monumentalism of bedsteads grew through the Victorian era to a high point in the 1880s. The scale of the bed makes it practically architecture, though this is a light and delicate set for its era. (Facing) This French lady's chair of the mid-nineteenth century sits waiting for the mistress of the house to put on her hose and shoes. The lamp table is late Empire in the style of the 1840s or '50s. The kerosene lamp is exotic in inspiration and probably 1870s or '80s in date.

It is in the 1870s that government was first mobilized as a force in the social purity movement. Until 1874 and the Comstock Act, government seldom got involved in questions of obscenity, vice, or abortion. Traditionally, life was thought to begin at quickening, that is when the mother can feel the fetus move. Midwives, homeopaths, pharmacists, and a host of other practitioners gave some type of medical care, including contraceptives and abortions, and were considered as legitimate as doctors. Only in the late nineteenth century did medical doctors consolidate their position and drive the competition out of business.

In the last third of the nineteenth century, most states outlawed abortion, outlawed contraception, outlawed pornography, and cracked down on prostitution. The Social Purity Movement mobilized the newly legitimate medical profession, the brand-new field of social work, and the Protestant evangelical movement to persuade government to act to regulate sexuality. For the first time in many places, adultery and premarital sex, homosexuality, and even contraception within marriage became illegal rather than just sinful.

On the lighter side, the Victorians' obsession with sex often looks

The lady's writing desk and chair are machine-made and Renaissance Revival in style. They were built in a factory and possibly transported long distances by railroad. Those forces were changing life forever while this classical, orderly house was being built. (Right) Bed canopies have no practical purpose by the late nineteenth century. These are just beautiful.

awfully silly to modern eyes. If a person looks for sexual innuendo, he is sure to find it, and late Victorians looked as hard as they could. Who but the perversely prudish would invent pantaloons for piano legs lest the delicate-minded be offended by the sight of bare legs? Legs, by the way, couldn't be mentioned in mixed company just in case the word brought to mind human legs, and heaven knows where thoughts of legs might lead. Legs were rechristened "limbs" as in a four-limbed table or a three-limbed stool.

The Victorian bedroom was pre-eminently a "man's room." Modern folk often put ruffles and roses in the bedroom as it seems appropriately

womanly in an otherwise gender-neutral house. In the late nineteenth century, however, most bedrooms were aggressively male. Huge, dark, Renaissance Revival beds had bucks and birds carved into the bedsteads, the furniture had hairy-paw feet, and the general atmosphere was heavy with hormones.

In the eighteenth and early nineteenth century, canopies on beds often included curtains which were closed to keep heat in at night. People were dependent on fireplaces for warmth and worked hard to keep away cold drafts. By the late nineteenth century, coal or wood parlor

stoves were common, and even central heating furnaces were available. The half-testers sometimes found on late Victorian beds are purely for decoration—most beds had no curtains at all. During the summer, especially in the South, mosquito nets were often suspended over beds. During the 1880s, "bug bars," that is machine-made wire window screens, were introduced and replaced the mosquito net for most people.

(Left and facing) The architectural character of 1880s Renaissance Revival beds is amply illustrated here at the Mainstay Inn. When it was Jackson's Clubhouse, the men gambling downstairs had use of the bedrooms upstairs.

SWEAT AND SELF-IMAGE

Daisy, Daisy, give me your answer, do!

I'm half crazy, all for the love of you!

It won't be a stylish marriage,

I can't afford a carriage,

But you'll look sweet upon the seat

Of a bicycle built for two!

—"Daisy Bell," 1892, Harry Dacre

ADJACENT TO THE VICTORIAN BEDROOM was an architectural feature that speaks of a deep and strong current in Victorian culture. The feature is the sleeping porch, and the current is, surprisingly enough, an obsession with health and fitness. We often think of ourselves as body-conscious, exercise fans and our nineteenth-century forebears as pot-bellied, port-drinking pudges. It isn't so.

One of the side effects of the urbanization of America was a sudden increase in communicable diseases. Remember that this was before the pure food and drug act, before people knew about the germ theory of disease, and before most people had access to refrigeration. Tainted water, food, and medicine were a serious problem. Tenements, streetcars, and railroads encouraged tuberculosis, smallpox, impetigo, yellow fever, and a host of other infections.

City dwellers knew that country folk were healthier. They didn't know why, but they saw that people who got a lot of fresh air and did physical work didn't catch tuberculosis and yellow fever as often. They reasoned that breathing used air was unhealthy, that the life-supporting oxygen had been depleted. They became fresh-air fiends. As often as weather permitted,

(Facing) These sleeping porches allowed Victorians to breathe unlimited sea air while they slumbered. Late-nineteenth-century requirements for fresh air were many times the modern minimum.

Victorians took to their sleeping porches at night. They established mountain resorts in the Adirondacks of New York, the Berkshires in Massachusetts, and the Appalachians of North Carolina. They flocked to the shore, founding beach towns such as Cape May, Atlantic City, and Ocean Grove in New Jersey, Pensacola in Florida, and Galveston in Texas. Victorians traveled to the shore to promenade in the fresh ocean air and wade in the surf. Swimming was a newly developed skill. Women wore linen bathing dresses and sometimes waded inside floating bathing tents for the sake of modesty. After all, Amelia Bloomer was just inventing women's underwear, and the wide bathing dresses tended to balloon up.

Everywhere, Victorians took to their bicycles. First, the penny-farthing appeared with its huge front wheel and tiny rear wheel. This proved to be dangerous sport as the penny-farthing tends to pitch the cyclist forward onto his head. Afterward, the development of the safety bicycle, with

(Left and facing) Victorians escaped to the mountains, leaving the tuberculosis and yellow fever of New York behind. The fresh climate of the Shawangunks can be found here at Mohonk Mountain House where the tradition of mountain getaways for weary Manhattanites continues.

two wheels of the same size and a seat between, made the new method of transportation a sensation. In America and in England, middle-class people pedaled their way to work and to play. In fact, the middle class adopted bicycles so wholeheartedly that upper-class people in Britain won't use them to this day.

Victorian exercise wasn't just limited to bicycles and beaches, however. It included the newly popular games of tennis, badminton, croquet, baseball, and softball. People took to weightlifting and tossing Indian clubs around. There were medicine balls, calisthenics, gymnastics, dumbbells, and barbells for ladies and gentlemen. The Victorian man worked up a sweat; however, the genteel Victorian woman would never sweat; she "glowed" instead. All this new activity required new wardrobes: tennis whites and golf plus-fours, newly invented bathing suits (pre-Victorians just skinny-dipped), cycling trousers for men, and even "rational garments" (trousers) for

(Facing) This Adirondack-style boathouse of the Silver Bay Association at Lake George is in a style originating in Upper New York state but equally at home in the Rockies or the Blue Ridge mountains. (Right) Italianate cupolas at the beach didn't just add that Renaissance touch, they ventilated the building, exhausting hot air from the top of the house.

women. Victorians weren't so many years removed from manual farm labor that they didn't realize they were getting out of shape. They threw themselves into exercise body and soul.

With all the emphasis on sex, just what *was* considered attractive in the late nineteenth century? For women in the 1840s and '50s, the Greek mode was widely favored. A slight figure with a small bosom and narrow hips was considered very elegant. Hair parted in the center and

worn close to the head forming curls or flaps in the back was the latest in Grecian fashion. Empire-waisted dresses were light, sometimes to the point of transparency, and necklines could be very low.

As the century progressed, the ideal figure became increasingly voluptuous with as much contrast as possible between wasp waists and full hips and busts. Women padded their buttocks and wore whale-bone corsets laced so tightly as to damage kidneys and ribs. Among the ultrafashionable, some women even had their lower ribs removed to create the ideal eighteen-inch waist. This was quite an extraordinary sacrifice considering that neither modern anesthetics nor antiseptics had yet been invented.

By the very late nineteenth century, women were supposed to be well padded indeed. During the 1880s, the bustle developed and grew larger every year. Essentially a wire or wicker basket tied to the waist and extending like a shelf off the back, the bustle lent an odd tilt to the figure. In the 1880s and '90s, a woman's figure when clothed consisted of a normally placed, though tightly confined, bosom, a narrow waist, and a shelf off the back. By the turn of the century, the bosom had dropped about a foot and was no longer tightly confined in a bodice. Instead, a loose, "man-tailored" blouse pulled out at the waist created a pigeon-breasted look. The com-

(Facing) Indoor plumbing was quite a luxury when this Lyndhurst bathroom was built. (Right) Patent medicines were part of the late Victorian's fevered search for a healthier life. Unfortunately, before the Pure Food and Drug Act was enacted, many were either ineffective or positively poisonous.

bination of this bowed front and bulging backside created the well-known Gibson Girl, s-shaped figures.

As long as poor people still worked outside at manual labor or farming, a tan was not considered attractive. Throughout the nineteenth century, men and women prized pale, unburned skin. During the very late nineteenth century, there even arose a fashion for taking arsenic. Small quantities of arsenic wouldn't kill the fashionable young woman but would give her complexion a refined, blue-white pallor that simply reeked of class.

Men, as usual, had it a lot easier. The eighteenth-century fashion of colorful, tight knickers and stockings still prevailed in the early nineteenth century. A man was supposed to be trim with well-developed calves and slim ankles. Whatever his figure, it was evident to the viewer as clothing was skin tight. As the century progressed, men's clothing got looser and more somber. Men's figures got stouter and stouter. By the late century, a

Performing one's toilette involved unguents and creams, but nineteenth-century women didn't wear makeup unless they were actresses or worse. (Facing) This "cottage style" washstand was what most people used instead of plumbing. This particularly lovely scene is in a summer bedroom at Acorn Hall in Morristown, New Jersey.

man was supposed to look "substantial" and well-fed. This was another way for the middle class to display its prosperity. As long as hunger was still a recent memory, stout men were considered attractive.

A curious side to Victorian wardrobes is the rarity of closets. With all these huge dresses and bustles, why are there so few closets in a Victorian bedroom, and why are they so small? There is a widespread myth that homeowners were charged property tax based on the number of closets in the house. This was never true. The real explanation for the scarcity of closets is the abundance of servants. The lady of the house would leave a card on her vanity describing the evening's outfit, and her maid would retrieve the clothes from an upstairs room where they were packed in chests of drawers, armoires, and boxes. The maid would steam or iron the clothes and lay them out on the bed ready to be put on. There was no incentive for making clothes storage convenient as long as someone else fetched them. Anyone with enough money for a substantial wardrobe also had servants and extra rooms for storage.

(Facing) Even the wealthy had little built-in clothing storage, as can be seen here in the Victoria Mansion. (Right) A man's outfit included numerous buttons, stays, collars, accessories, and specialized boxes to store them in. Here they are displayed on a dresser at Leith Hall.

"What ho, Jeeves," I cried, entering the room where he waded knee-deep in suitcases and shirts and winter-suitings, like a sea-beast among rocks. "Packing?"

"Yes Sir," replied the honest fellow, for there are no secrets between us.

—*Very Good Jeeves,* 1930, P. G. Wodehouse

COLLECTING MANIA

It is through Art, and through Art only, that we can realize our
perfection; through Art and Art only that we can shield
ourselves from the sordid perils of actual existence.

—1890, Oscar Wilde

(Pages 116-117)
Frederick Church
premiered the artist's
home studio as a
"bohemian expres-
sion" of his Aesthetic
personality. Most of
these home studios
were found in
England, owned
by pioneers such as
William Morris and
Burne-Jones, but
Church brought the
phenomena to the
shores of the Hudson.
(Facing) Never hav-
ing heard modernist
Le Corbusier's dictum
of "Less is more,"
Victorians thought
more was just about
enough.

THE COLLECTING MANIA that is so evident in Victorian houses is a function of the new conditions of life in the nineteenth century and, at the same time, a reaction against this modern life.

The Industrial Revolution made collecting mania possible. In the early nineteenth century, silver was expensive and handmade. By the late Victorian era, electroplating made silver plate accessible to almost everyone. In the early nineteenth century, glass and china were dear; by the end of the century, they were cheap. In the early century, iron was hand wrought; by the end, there was factory-made cast-iron. In the beginning, there was ivory; by the end, there was nitro-cellulose plastic.

The Industrial Revolution made collecting mania possible in another way, too. At the beginning of the nineteenth century, the wealthy had their possessions handmade and passed them down from generation to generation. By the end of the century, most Americans would have called themselves middle-class. There was a large body of white-collar, office workers who labored for wages and could afford to buy material goods. They certainly hadn't inherited old family silver and china from their farmer parents. As one wag has observed, it's better to buy your

heirlooms anyway, that way you can get exactly what you want.

The flood of cheap, machine-made goods produced a powerful reaction. Suddenly, Aesthetic Movement tastemakers had lots of people agreeing with their belief that modern taste had been degraded. There was a new cachet to the handmade and the primitive now that everything wasn't handmade by necessity. The adjective "natural" became desirable and romantic. Rocks and minerals, dried flowers and ferns, stuffed birds and animals, shells and exotic plants—all these were classified and displayed in the Victorian house.

Inexpensive travel by railroad and steamships permitted a fad for souvenirs and exotica. Statuettes of the newly erected Eiffel Tower, the Statue of Liberty, and the Brooklyn Bridge honored these marvels of modern engineering. Leaning towers of Pisa and St. Peter's basilicas memorialized the classical world, while Navajo pots and Egyptian shards proclaimed their owners as familiar with exotic cultures.

All exotic cultures, especially pre-industrial ones, were highly respected. A collection of Japanese and Turkish knickknacks was evidence that its owner knew that modern industrial design was dross compared with real handicrafts made by "unspoiled" natives. Aesthetes might arrange their souvenirs in artful still lifes.

A sidelight to this love of collections is the Victorian love of labeling and categorizing. Often Victorians lined things up in their collections and named each piece. Display cases were filled with neatly labeled minerals instead of a lush, random arrangement in the aesthetic manner. Organizing nature can be seen as an extension of the Industrial Revolution, wherein

(Facing) Here at Lyndhurst, Jay Gould could imagine himself a modern Maecenas collecting the most valuable art. (Right) While the hoi polloi collected machine-made knick-knacks, Frederick Church collected fine art and handmade exotica at Olana.

man harnesses nature's power of steam, coal, and iron. Organizing and taking control of one's surroundings can be seen as the popular version of the advancement of science in the nineteenth century.

The collecting mania of the late 1800s was part of a new materialism that was found in every area of life. The new, realistic novel was a product of the nineteenth century. Henry James and Marcel Proust are famous for their careful observation of details: tastes, smells, objects, clothing. Attaching more significance to things and to the world of the five senses and de-emphasizing abstract principles is a peculiarly Victorian characteristic. Think of Sherlock Holmes coming upon an object and deducing the character, position, and origin of the person who used it: a gentleman, recently in India, of good character but under a great strain, married but living apart from his wife, etc. This is certainly the extreme example of the Victorians' faith in the object as a mirror of its owner. No wonder they took such care to create a good impression with the right objects.

During the eighteenth-century Enlightenment, the reaction to an

(Left and facing) Victorian collections are eclectic above all, but there are definitely themes. The group on the left illustrates the pretty, floriferous, feminine school, while that on the right represents the hand-made, exotic, and "tasteful."

object of beauty was always described as cool, spiritual, detached. By the late nineteenth century it was a lust to own it. The old aristocratic ability to unite one's soul with the beauties of art was gone. Instead there was the middle-class reaction of "I see it, I like it, I want it." The department store was the institution to satisfy that lust. As Marshall Field of Chicago said, "Give the lady what she wants." Early department-store magnates had to overcome the traditional view that marketing is a job and a burden. They did all they could to make shopping an entertainment. In 1878, Macy's and Wanamakers in New York had that clever New Jerseyite, Thomas Edison, install electric lights. Strawbridge and Clothiers in Philadelphia had Mr. Otis install his new elevator years before, and New York entrepreneurs such as Cooper Siegel and Lord & Taylor needed to catch up with electric versions in the 1880s. Marshall Field's in Chicago installed pneumatic tubes in 1893 to speed back the customer's change. In downtown Manhattan, John Wanamaker pioneered the department store designed as a palace, and all his competitors vied with each other for the greatest old master paintings to

display, the tallest columns, the most brilliant chandeliers. These modern Medicis invited the customer into their cast-iron palazzi and bid the customer to take home a little of their magnificence.

The most extreme object-worship was embodied by Oscar Wilde who, faced with an exquisitely designed teapot, said he "hoped he could live up to it." His precious, aesthetic reaction was greeted with hoots of derision. Royal Worcester china memorialized the incident with the Oscar Wilde teapot: hand on hip forming the handle and limp wrist forming the spout. Wilde may have been the extreme, but many people equated good design with goodness in character and gave taste great importance.

(Facing and right) At Olana, the overwhelming impression is that of a Middle-Eastern bazaar with caravans just unpacking treasures from the fabled East. This mixed Levantine style is what Frederick Church called "Personal Persian."

THE TWENTIETH CENTURY

HOW IS THE TWENTIETH CENTURY different from the nineteenth? In many ways, the early twentieth century was no different. Many historians end the nineteenth century with World War I which finished much of the old order of European royalty. In architecture, there were a few new things that began just around the turn of the century: the Colonial Revival style and the open plan, the Arts and Crafts movement, and the steel-frame skyscraper.

Several movements in the late nineteenth century continued into the twentieth and took new forms. The Aesthetic Movement rejected the froufrou, French aesthetic of the Industrial Revolution and looked to the Middle Ages for a handmade alternative. When Eastlake furniture was coopted by furniture manufacturers, the same impulse was reborn as the Arts and Crafts movement. The Arts and Crafts movement championed honest, handmade, oak furniture with honest, hand-forged or beaten hardware. Instead of the style of the Middle Ages, they revived the craft and artisanship of the Middle Ages. Gustave Stickley, the prophet of the Arts and Crafts movement, even founded utopian worker's villages hoping to revive the paternalistic master and apprentice relationship of olden times. The elegant furniture conceived by Stickley was made with big copper hinges and oak sections undisguised by varnish. Of course, Stickley didn't reckon on the power of capitalism after the Industrial Revolution, and his utopian dreams went the way of Eastlake's. Mass-produced knock-offs poured off the assembly lines of Grand Rapid's factories and made Arts and Crafts furniture the modern choice for bungalows across the continent.

Another late nineteenth-century style that continued and flourished

(Pages 126-127)
Early twentieth-century Colonial Revival houses are possibly the most gracious dwellings ever built— eighteenth-century proportion with light, air, and a scale suited to modern life. After the stock market crash in 1929, houses like this have seldom been seen again. (Facing) The intense color and matte glaze of Rockwood and Roycroft pottery represented the lost crafts of the Middle Ages for the tasteful collectors of the early twentieth century.

in the early twentieth century was the Colonial Revival. During the late 1880s and '90s, one of the reactions against the Industrial Revolution was a turn toward the pre-industrial 1700s. At first this revival of colonial-era design was very loose and sketchy. The same sorts of houses that might be Queen Anne style would also be Colonial Revival. Asymmetrical, with a corner tower and wraparound porch, the early Colonial Revival house differed from the Queen Anne only in using Georgian motifs.

One of the great developments in house planning that took place in Colonial Revival houses around 1900 is the open plan. Most Victorian houses were conceived of as a series of rooms, a group of boxes aligned along a hall. The open plan house is conceived of as a space, modified and modulated by walls, screens, pocket doors, etc. A large stairhall might be open to the parlor with only a couple of columns to mark the separation, and the parlor might be open to the dining room with a screen or arch or large pocket doors making the separation. Frank Lloyd Wright designed the most sophisticated, open-plan houses of the earlier twentieth century. His work marks a distinct breaking point between the traditional, domestic

The Arts & Crafts Movement's reverence for the hand wrought is deserved in this collection of early twentieth-century art glass by Louis Comfort Tiffany. It is displayed on a Tiffany & Company sideboard at Evergreen House in Baltimore and represents the acme of craftmanship in American history.

architecture of the nineteenth century and modern, domestic architecture of the twentieth. Seen one way, Wright was certainly revolutionary in his advancement of the open-plan house. Seen another, he was very much a man of his time in his designs for a variation on Arts and Crafts furniture and his subscription to the Romantic Movement's love of natural materials.

The early Colonial Revival house was often filled with Colonial Revival furniture that was just as free an interpretation of eighteenth-century furniture as the house was loosely based on real colonial houses. As the twentieth century wore on, the houses developed much more arch-aeologically correct, porchless, symmetrical facades with six-over-six windows and Federal dormers. The furniture also moved closer to the eighteenth century with reproduction Chippendale and Queen Anne suites and true colonial antiques.

To go back to our Victorian people in their Victorian houses, their secret is that they were modern people with at least as much social dislocation and stress as we have. Imagine an office worker in New York City in 1904. He would live in an apartment building furnished with indoor plumbing and electricity. He'd get up in the morning, put on a suit, and commute to work on the new subway train. The office was in a steel-framed office building lit by electricity, complete with elevators, typewriters, and Dictaphones. He'd eat lunch at a fast-food lunch counter and go home by subway or perhaps go out to dinner in one of those new "bohemian" restaurants in Greenwich Village or an Italian restaurant on Mulberry Street. It doesn't sound very different from an office worker's day today. Most of the wrenching changes in daily life had already happened by 1904, and daily life hasn't really changed that radically since then.

Our look at Victorian houses has shown that the many styles and motifs we see in Victorian design had profound meaning for people at the time. Our nostalgic images of cozy comfort, ruffles, and roses are not the whole picture and shouldn't obscure both the richness and the conflicts of late nineteenth-century life. Their interests and concerns, which are so similar to our own, demonstrate that Victorians were more like us than any previous generation.

America is the noisiest country that ever existed. One is waked up in the morning, not by the singing of the nightingale, but by the steam whistle. It is surprising that the sound practical sense of the Americans does not reduce this intolerable noise.

—Impressions of America, 1883, Oscar Wilde

(Facing) The elegance of the early twentieth-century Colonial Revival is demonstrated in this Charleston, South Carolina, single house. All the elements are eighteenth century but used with an abundance not found until 1900.

BIBLIOGRAPHY

Boorstin, Daniel J. *The Americans: The National Experience*. New York: Random House, 1965.

Burke, Doreen Bolger, et al. *In Pursuit of Beauty: Americans and the Aesthetic Movement*. New York: The Metropolitan Museum of Art; Rizzoli International Publications, 1986.

Calder, Jenni. *Women and Marriage in Victorian Fiction*. New York: Oxford University Press, 1976.

D'Emilio, John, and Estelle B. Freedman. *Intimate Matters: A History of Sexuality in America*. New York: Harper & Row, Publishers, 1988.

Downing, Andrew Jackson. *Cottage Residences; | or, | A Series of Designs|for|Rural Cottages and Cottage Villas, | and their | Gardens and Grounds. | Adapted to | North America*. 1873. Rpt. as *Victorian Cottage Residences*. New York: Dover Publications, 1981.

Dresser, Christopher. *The Art of Decorative Design*. 1862. Watkins Glen: The American Life Foundation & Study Institute, 1977.

Eastlake, Charles L. *Hints on Household Taste in Furniture, Upholstery and Other Details*. 1878. Rpt. as *Hints on Household Taste: The Classic Handbook of Victorian Interior Decoration*. New York: Dover Publications, 1986.

Farb, Peter and George Armelagos. *Consuming Passions: The Anthropology of Eating*. Boston: Houghton Mifflin Company, 1980.

Fitch, James Marston. *American Building 1: The Historical Forces that Shaped It*. 2nd ed. New York: Schocken Books, 1973.

Fraser, Antonia. *The Weaker Vessel*. New York: Alfred A. Knopf, 1984.

Gernsheim, Alison. *Fashion and Reality (1840-1914)*. 1963. Rpt. as *Victorian & Edwardian Fashion: A Photographic Survey*. New York: Dover Publications, 1981.

Gist, Noel P. and Sylvia Fleis Fava. *Urban Society*. 5th ed. New York: Thomas Y. Crowell Company, 1964.

Kasson, John F. *Rudeness & Civility: Manners in Nineteenth-Century Urban America*. New York: Farrar, Straus and Giroux, 1990.

McGee, Harold. *On Food and Cooking: The Science and Lore of the Kitchen*. New York: Charles Scribner's Sons, 1984.

Pierson, William H., Jr. *American Buildings and Their Architects: The Colonial and Neoclassical Styles*. 1970. Garden City: Anchor Books, 1976.

Revel, Jean-Francois. *Culture and Cuisine: A Journey Through the History of Food*. Trans. Helen R. Lane. 1982. New York: Da Capo Press, 1984.

Root, Waverley, and Richard de Rochemont. *Eating in America: A History*. New York: The Ecco Press, 1981.

Root, Waverley. *Food: An Authoritative, Visual History and Dictionary of the Foods of the World.* New York: Simon & Schuster, 1980.

Saisselin, Remy G. *Bricabracomania: The Bourgeois and the Bibelot.* London: Thames and Hudson Ltd., 1985.

Schlereth, Thomas J. *Victorian America: Transformations in Everyday Life, 1876-1915.* The Everyday Life in America Ser. New York: HarperCollins Publishers, 1991.

Schlesinger, Arthur Meier. *The Rise of the City, 1878-1898.* A History of American Life Ser. 10. 1933. Chicago: Quadrangle Books, 1971.

Shapiro, Laura. *Perfection Salad: Women and Cooking at the Turn of the Century.* New York: Farrar, Straus and Giroux, 1986.

Smith, Henry Nash. *Virgin Land: The American West as Symbol and Myth.* 1950. Reprint. New York: Alfred A. Knopf, Random House, n.d.

Tannahill, Reay. *Food in History.* New York: Crown Publishers, Inc., 1989.

—. *Sex in History.* New York: Stein and Day, 1980.

Trachtenberg, Alan, ed. *Democratic Vistas: 1860-1880.* The American Culture Ser. 4. New York: George Braziller, 1970.

Visser, Margaret. *Much Depends on Dinner: The Extraordinary History and Mythology, Allure and Obsessions, Perils and Taboos of an Ordinary Meal.* New York: Collier Books Macmillan Publishing Company, 1986.

—. *The Rituals of Dinner: The Origins, Evolution, Eccentricities, and Meaning of Table Manners.* New York: Grove Weidenfeld, 1991.

Wade, Richard C. *The Urban Frontier: The Rise of Western Cities, 1790-1830.* 1959. Rpt as *The Urban Frontier: Pioneer Life in Early Pittsburgh, Cincinnati, Lexington, Louisville, and St. Louis.* Chicago: University of Chicago Press, n.d.

Wharton, Edith and Ogden Codman, Jr. *The Decoration of Houses.* 1902. New York: W. W. Norton & Company, 1978.

SOURCE LIST

Old House Journal Magazine
P.O. Box 420235
Palm Coast, FL 32142-0235
800-234-3797
www.oldhousejournal.com
The best source list for materials and craftsmen is the Old House Journal Directory. *Published annually by* Old House Journal Magazine, *it can also be referenced on line.*

☞ Cast Iron

Moultrie Manufacturing Company
P.O. Box 2948
Moultrie, GA 31776-1179
912-985-1312
Some nice Victorian castings made into some truly awful pastiche fences.

☞ Ceiling Fans

Hunter Fan Company
2500 Frisco Avenue
Memphis, TN 38114
901-743-1360
Hunter makes one 1880s reproduction ceiling fan.

☞ Ceiling Medallions / Moldings

Focal Point
3006 Anaconda Road
Tarboro, NC 27886
800-662-5550
These are the manufacturers of the expanded, polystyrene cornices and other architectural trim you see everywhere. Their own catalog has a better selection than elsewhere.

Soltis Plastering
Box 4, 121 Basswood
Upsala, MN 56384
320-573-4952
Ornamental plaster cornices, rosettes, and other architectural trim.

W. T. Weaver & Sons Inc.
1208 Wisconsin Avenue NW
Washington, D.C. 20007
202-333-4200
Astonishingly inexpensive ceiling medallions made of styrene.

☞ Exterior Lighting

Park Place
2251 Wisconsin Avenue NW
Washington, D.C. 20007
202-342-6294
Interesting street lamps, sconces, etc.

☞ Flooring

Bangkok International
4562 Worth Street
Philadelphia, PA 19124
215-537-5800
Gorgeous parquet flooring and borders.

☞ Gardens

Milaeger's Gardens
4838 Douglas Avenue
Racine, WI 53402-2498
800-669-1229
Their "Perennial Wish Book" is one of the most complete catalogs of modern and old-fashioned flowers.

Pinetree Garden Seeds
P.O. Box 300
New Gloucester, ME 04260
207-926-3400
The best source for hard-to-find seeds for antique vegetables, and they sell in tiny quantities for home gardeners.

Wayside Gardens
One Garden Lane
Hodges, SC 29695-0001
800-845-1124
The great source for old-fashioned roses (hybrid perpetuals and bourbons) from the late nineteenth century.

☞ Gilt

Art Essentials of N.Y. Ltd.
25 Church Road
Monsey, NY 10952
800-283-5323
Gilding supplies.

☞ Hardware

Anglo-American Brass Co.
P.O. Drawer 9487
San Jose, CA 95157-9487
408-246-3232
An inexpensive selection of cabinet, door, and plumbing hardware.

The Antique Hardware Store
19 Buckingham Plantation Drive
Bluffton, SC 29910
800-422-9982
www.antiquehardware.com
Mostly plumbing and some cabinet hardware.

Arvid's Woods
2500 Hewitt Avenue
Everett, WA 98201
425-252-8374
Manufacturer of gaskets for doors and windows.

Ball & Ball
463 West Lincoln Highway
Exton, PA 19341
610-363-7330 (outside PA 800-257-3711)
Hinges and door hardware, well made and expensive.

Classic Accents, Inc.
P.O. Box 1181
Southgate, MI 48195
734-941-8011
Brass, push-button light-switch covers.

Paxton Hardware
P.O. Box 256
7818 Bradshaw Road
Upper Falls, MD 21156
410-592-8505
A great hardware catalog with special products for adapting old lamps.

The Renovators Supply
Miller Falls, MA 01349
800-659-2211
Their sales offer sinks and other fixtures cheaper than anywhere else.

Interior Lighting

B & P Lamp Supply
843 Old Morrison Highway
McMinnville, TN 37110
931-473-3016
Wholesale distributor and manufacturer of lamp parts, lamp components, and lamp shades.

Kings Chandelier Co.
Highway 14
P.O. Box 667-SLV
Eden, NC 27288
336-623-6188
A wide variety of crystal chandeliers, including a few convincing 1860s–70s gaslight models.

Nowell's Lighting
P.O. Box 295
490 Gate Five Road at Harbor Drive
Sausalito, CA 94966
415-332-4933
Reproduction chandeliers and sconces.

Lace

J. R. Burrows & Co.
393 Union Street
Rockland, MA 02370
781-982-1812
Authentic Victorian lace panels.

Millwork

Allegheny Restoration
P.O. Box 18032
Morgantown, WV 26507
304-594-2570
Specializing in the restoration of windows and doors as well as custom millwork. Will make doors and windows to match historic profiles. Free literature.

Anthony Wood Products
P.O. Box 1081
113 Industrial Loop
Hillsboro, TX 76645
254-582-7225
A wide selection of gingerbread.

Crawford's Old House Store
W1508 Marsh Road
Palmyra, WI 53156
414-495-3107
Turned, wooden corner protectors that were so common in Victorian cottages.

The Emporium Inc.
1800 Westheimer Road
Houston, TX 77098
713-528-3808
A nice selection of spindle screens and brackets.

Mad River Woodworks
P.O. Box 1067
189 Taylor Way
Blue Lake, CA 95525-1067
707-668-5671
Well-made and low-priced roof shingles and gingerbread trim.

Mendecino Millwork
Box 669
Mendecino, CA 95460
707-937-4410
Redwood millwork including baseboards, door and window casings.

San Francisco Victoriana
2070 Newcomb Avenue
San Francisco, CA 94124
415-648-0313
The best Victorian molding catalog I know.

Silverton Victorian Millworks
P.O. Box 2987
Durango, CO 81302
970-259-5915
800-933-3930
A good millwork catalog with hard-to-find, fancy-cut roof shingles.

Vintage Wood Works
P.O. Box 39
9195 Highway 34 South
Quinlan, TX 75474
903-356-2158
A really good Victorian millwork catalog similar in scope to Anthony Wood Products.

✸ Mold Making

Polytek
55 Hilton Street
Easton, PA 18042
610-559-8620
A source for rubbery stuff to make molds of existing architectural features to cast reproductions.

✸ Plumbing

The Antique Plumber
885 57th Street
Sacramento, CA 95819
916-454-4507
A catalog of very nice but expensive Victorian plumbing supplies.

✸ Telephones

Phoneco, Inc.
P.O. Box 70
19813 East Mill Road
Galesville, WI 54630
608-582-4124
A wonderful source at reasonable cost for every kind of antique phone and for phone repair and restoration.

✸ Tile

Designs in Tile
P.O. Box 358, Dept. S
Mount Shasta, CA 96067
530-926-2629
www.designsintile.com
Nice Eastlake and Neo-Grec transfer tiles.

✸ Wallpaper and Paint

Bradbury & Bradbury
P.O. Box 155
940 Tyler Street, Suite 12
Benicia, CA 94510
707-746-1900

The single best source for reproductions and adaptations of Aesthetic Movement wallpaper designs.

Janovic Plaza
30-35 Thomson Avenue
Long Island City, NY 11101
718-786-4444
Janovic Plaza has joined with one of New York's oldest paint stores–Wolff Paints. They offer graining and marbleizing supplies, glazes, and a nice selection of classical column and entablature wallpapers.

Sanderson N.A.
979 Third Avenue, Suite 409
New York, NY 10022
Exclusive supplier of William Morris-designed wallpapers as well as other Morris period designs.

❧ Wood Shutters

Shuttercraft
282 Stepstone Hill Road
Guilford, CT 06437
203-453-1973
Movable louver and wooden shutters and hard-ware.

❧ Woodworking

Abatron
5501 95th Avenue
Kenosha, WI 53144
414-653-2000
Manufacturers of adhesives, wood consolidants, and wood replacement compounds.

Amherst Woodworking & Supply
30 Industrial Drive
Northampton, MA 01061
413-584-3003
Custom manufacturer of architectural woodworking.

Constantine's
2050 Eastchester Road
Bronx, NY 10461
800-223-8087
The best source for sophisticated wood-finishing supplies.

Lee Valley Tools
1090 Morrison Drive
Ottawa, Ontario K2H 1C2
Canada
613-596-0350
The most beautiful catalog of beautiful hand tools.

Leichtung Workshops
5604 Alameda Place NE
Albuquerque, NM 87113
800-645-9292
An impressive catalog and really neat tools.

PHOTOGRAPHY LIST AND ADDITIONAL HOUSE MUSEUMS

The Abbey Bed & Breakfast
Columbia Avenue & Gurney Street
Cape May, NJ 08204
609-884-4506
Photographs pages 4, 12, 26, 27, 40, 54, and 118.

Acorn Hall House Museum
68 Morris Avenue
Morristown, NJ 07960
973-267-3465
Photographs pages 30, 113, and 137.

The Audubon House
205 Whitehead Street
Key West, FL 33040
305-294-2116

The Banning Residence Museum
401 East M Street
Wilmington, CA 90748
310-548-7777

Henry Bowen House, Roseland Cottage
On the Common, Route 169
Woodstock, CT 06281
203-928-4074
Photographs pages 17, 65, 67, 69, and 139 lower.

Campbell House
1508 Locust Street
St. Louis, MO 63103
314-421-0325

Camron-Stanford House
1418 Lakeside Drive
Oakland, CA 94612
510-444-1876

The Columbia House
26 Ocean Street
Cape May, NJ 08204
609-884-2789
Photograph page 92.

COLVMNS BY THE SEA®
Bed & Breakfast
1513 Beach Drive
Cape May, NJ 08204
609-884-2228
Photographs page 122.

The Curry Mansion
511 Caroline Street
Key West, FL 33040
305-294-5349

Ebenezer Maxwell Mansion
200 West Tulpehocken Street
Philadelphia, PA 19144
215-438-1861
Photographs pages 7, 18, 28, 32, 42, and 45.

Edmonston-Alston House
21 East Battery
Charleston, SC 29401
843-722-7171
Photographs pages 85 and 86.

The Emlen Physick Estate
1048 Washington Street
Cape May, NJ 08204
609-884-5404
Photographs pages 33, 38, 39, 43, 94, and 95.

Evergreen House
The John Hopkins University
4545 North Charles Street
Baltimore, MD 21210
410-516-0341
Photographs pages 130 and 137.

The Fontaine House
680 Adams Avenue
Memphis, TN 38105
901-526-1469

Gallier House
1118-32 Royal Street
New Orleans, LA 70116
504-523-6722

Hay House
934 Georgia Avenue
Macon, GA 31201
912-742-8155

Historic General Dodge House
621 Third Street
Council Bluffs, IA 51505
712-322-2406

Honolulu House
107 North Kalamazoo Street
Marshall, MI 49068
616-781-8544

Iolani Palace
Friends of Iolani Palace
P.O. Box 2259
Honolulu, HI 96804
808-522-0832

Leith Hall
Historic Seashore Inn
22 Ocean Street
Cape May, NJ 08204
609-884-1934
Photographs pages 44 and 115.

Lyndhurst
A Property of the National Trust for Historic
Preservation
635 South Broadway
Tarrytown, NY 10591
914-631-4481
*Photographs pages 8–9, 21, 51, 62, 64, 66, 110,
112, 120, and 123.*

Mackenzie House
82 Bond Street
Toronto, Ontario M5B 1X2
Canada
416-392-6915

The Mainstay Bed & Breakfast
635 Columbia Avenue
Cape May, NJ 08204
609-884-8690
Photographs pages 20, 72, 73, 102, and 103.

Maymont House
1700 Hampton Street
Richmond, VA 23220
804-358-7166

The Molly Brown House Museum
1340 Pennsylvania Street
Denver, CO 80203
303-832-4092

Mohonk Mountain House
A National Historic Landmark
Lake Mohonk, New Paltz, NY 12561
914-255-1000
Photographs pages 106 and 107.

The Moody Mansion & Museum
2618 Broadway Avenue
Galveston, TX 77550
409-762-7668

Olana State Historic Site
New York State Office of Parks, Recreation,
and Historic Preservation, Taconic Region
RD 2
Hudson, NY 12534
518-828-0135
*Photographs pages 46–47, 48, 49, 116-117, 121,
124, 125, 134, and 140.*

Old Merchant's House
29 East Fourth Street
New York, NY 10003
212-777-1089
Photographs pages 55, 58, and 60.

Park-McCullough House
P.O. Box 388
Corner Park & West Streets
North Bennington, VT 05257
802-442-5441
*Photographs pages 74, 75, 96, 98, 99, 100, 101,
and 111.*

The Queen Victoria
102 Ocean Street
Cape May, NJ 08204
609-884-8702
Photographs pages 128 and 131.

Rockwood Museum
610 Shipley Road
Wilmington, DE 19809
302-761-4340
Photographs pages 1, 31, and 90–91.

Rutherford House
11153 Saskatchewan Drive
Edmonton, Alberta T6G 2S1
Canada
403-427-3995

The Shadows-on-the-Teche
A Property of the National Trust for Historic
Preservation
317 East Main Street
New Iberia, LA 70560
318-369-6446

Shand House
P.O. Box 2683
389 Avon Street
Windsor, Nova Scotia BON 2T0
Canada
902-798-5619
Open June 1 to October 15.

Spadina
285 Spadina Road
Toronto, Ontario M5R 2V5
Canada
416-392-6910

Taylor-Grady House
634 Price Avenue
Athens, GA 30601
706-549-8688
Photographs pages 57, 61, and 82.

Terrace Hill
(Governor's Residence)
2300 Grand Avenue
Des Moines, IA 50312
515-281-3604

Ulysses S. Grant Home
State Historic Site
500 Bouthillier Street
Galena, IL 61036
815-777-0248

Victoria Mansion
109 Danforth Street
Portland, ME 04101
207-772-4841
Photographs pages 10, 22–23, 34, 35, 37, 50, 76, 114, and 139 upper.

Wilderstein Preservation
Morton Road
Rhinebeck, NY 12572
914-876-4818
Photographs pages 24, 36, and 68.

Windward House
Bed & Breakfast
24 Jackson Street
Cape May, NJ 08204
609-884-3368
Photograph page 15.

☎ For heritage properties in Victoria, British Columbia, contact:

Heritage Branch
Ministry of Tourism and Culture
800 Johnson Street
Victoria, B.C. V8V 1X4
Canada
250-356-1432

☎ For listings of Victorian house museums in England, contact:

Historic Houses Association
2 Chester Street
London SW1X 7BB
England
207-259-5688

Victorian Society
One Priority Gardens
London W4 ITT
England
208-994-1019

ACKNOWLEDGMENTS

We would like to thank some of the many people who helped with this book—Jay and Marianne Schatz at The Abbey, Tom and Sue Carroll at the Mainstay, Barry Rein at COLVMNS BY THE SEA, Joan and Dane Wells at the Queen Victoria, B. Michael Zuckerman, the Director of the Mid-Atlantic Center for the Arts, and Diane Kereluik, the curator of the Emlen Physick Estate, all of Cape May. Special thanks to Sandy Miller of Windward House for the use of her house and her splendid antique clothing, as well as her knowledge of how Victorians dressed; and special thanks to Barbara Daggett of Columbia House for the use of her house and for introducing us to Tim Fields. Thanks as well to Rena Leith for her supportive, professional reviewing of the manuscript. —E. & S. Z.-L.

I would like to thank those who made this book possible—the curators and directors of the lovingly and meticulously maintained house museums, for their enthusiasm and the latitude of exploration they afforded me in creating these images; and the innkeepers of Cape May, New Jersey, whose beautiful show of houses and hospitality sparked my interest in photographing Victorian architecture and interiors. A very special thanks to Barbara Daggett of Columbia House in Cape May, for her encouragement when this book was but an idea, and for introducing me to many wonderful people in Cape May, among them Elan and Susan Zingman-Leith, to whom I owe great thanks for accommodating me in their fascinating bed and breakfast and for the enlightening conversations about the Victorian era. Thanks most of all to my wife Karen, for her constant and essential support and for keeping our two-year-old son Alec happy while I traveled during an already busy time in her life. —T.F.